Healthcare Relationship Marketing

Healthcare Relationship Marketing

Strategy, Design and Measurement

IRA J. HAIMOWITZ

Routledge
Taylor & Francis Group

LONDON AND NEW YORK

First published in paperback 2024

First published 2011 by Gower Publishing

Published 2016 by Routledge
4 Park Square, Milton Park, Abingdon, Oxon OX14 4RN

and by Routledge
605 Third Avenue, New York, NY 10158

Routledge is an imprint of the Taylor & Francis Group, an informa business

Publisher's Note
The publisher has gone to great lengths to ensure the quality of this reprint but points out that some imperfections in the original copies may be apparent.

British Library Cataloguing in Publication Data
Haimowitz, Ira J.
  Healthcare relationship marketing : strategy, design and
  measurement.
  1. Pharmaceutical industry--Management. 2. Drugs--
  Marketing. 3. Relationship marketing. 4. Brand loyalty.
  I. Title
  615.1'0688-dc22

Library of Congress Cataloging-in-Publication Data
Haimowitz, Ira J.
  Healthcare relationship marketing : strategy, design and measurement / Ira J. Haimowitz.
     p. cm.
  Includes bibliographical references and index.
  ISBN 978-0-566-09217-6 (hbk.) 1. Drugs--Marketing. 2. Relationship marketing.
  3. Pharmaceutical industry. I. Title.
  HD9665.5.H35 2010
  615.1068'8--dc22

                                                                            2010043842

ISBN: 978-0-566-09217-6 (hbk)
ISBN: 978-1-03-283839-7 (pbk)
ISBN: 978-1-315-58638-0 (ebk)

DOI: 10.4324/9781315586380

Contents

List of Figures

List of Tables

List of Abbreviations

APLD	Anonymous patient level data
AOL	America Online
ATU	Awareness, Trial, and Usage
BRC	Business reply card
CLM	Closed loop marketing
CLP	Closed loop promotion
CME	Continuing medical education
CPL	Cost per lead
CPQL	Cost per qualified lead
CPM	Cost per thousand impressions
CRM	Consumer relationship marketing
DB	Database
DDMAC	Division of Drug Marketing, Advertising, and Communications
DM	Direct (postal) mail
DMA	Direct Marketing Association
DR	Direct response
DRTV	Direct response television advertising
DTC	Direct to consumer advertising
ECOA	Email change of address
EM	Electronic mail (Email)
FDA	US Food and Drug Administration
GA	General awareness
GRP	Gross rating point
HCP	Healthcare professional
HIPAA	Health Insurance Portability and Accountability Act
IDI	In-depth interview
IVR	Interactive voice response
KOL	Key opinion leader
KPI	Key performance indicator
MCM	Multi-channel marketing
MOA	Mechanism of action
MVA	Master visual aid
NCOA	National change of address
NPP	Non-personal promotion

PCP   Primary care physican
PDA   Personal digital assistant
POA   Plan of action
PRM   Professional relationship marketing
RM   Relationship marketing
ROI   Return on investment
Rx   Prescription
SEM   Search engine marketing
SEO   Search engine optimization
SFA   Sales force automation
URL   Universal resource locator (website address)
WAC   Wholesale acquisition cost

About the Author

Ira Haimowitz is Senior Vice President/Group Director, Analytics and Operations at The CementBloc in New York City. Throughout his career, Ira has led teams providing healthcare clients innovative solutions for segmentation, targeting, measurement, and optimization. He has also enabled clients to evaluate the return on investment of their multi-channel consumer and professional advertising campaigns.

Previous to joining The CementBloc, Ira was Vice President/Group Director of Insights and Optimization at Wunderman Health. Ira has also spent nine years on the manufacturer side as a Director/Team Leader for pharmaceutical companies Pfizer and Organon. At Pfizer, Ira led a Data Innovation team that created the digital analytics practice for evaluating websites, banners, and search. Ira also spearheaded intelligent sales force targeting tools, including dashboards of medical group practices and integrated delivery systems. At Organon, Ira led the world-wide initiatives on sales force effectiveness, forecasting, and competitive intelligence. Ira previously worked for four years at General Electric Research and Development

Ira received his Ph.D. in Computer Science from the Massachusetts Institute of Technology in 1994, and previously an M. Phil. from Cambridge University in Computer Speech and Language Processing. He has spoken and published extensively, and has also served for seven years on the Board of the Pharmaceutical Management Science Association, including a tenure as President in 2006.

Ira is also the author of a long-running blog entitled Healthcare Relationship Marketing, which can be found at this Internet address: http://www.healthcarerm.blogspot.com

Ira lives with his wife Barbara, and children Nathan, Eva, and Deborah, in Riverdale, New York City.

Acknowledgements

I have benefited from working in several leading-edge, nurturing environments that have given me education and experience in pharmaceutical marketing and sales promotion. These include:

- The MIT Clinical Decision Making Group under Professor Peter Szolovits, where strong research was continually encouraged;

- General Electric, where I learned the value of applying technological innovation to practical problems, and being a business consultant;

- Pfizer, where I gained significant experience in pharmaceutical sales and marketing, Organon, where I learned to appreciate global marketing, pre-launch planning, and forecasting;

- Wunderman, which was a fertile ground for learning the details of multi-channel relationship marketing, and where Andrew Sexton, Margie Chiu, and Toni Iacono all lent advice and support. Becky Chidester and Mark Taylor of Wunderman both agreed to be industry experts for this book as well;

- The CementBloc, which has been a nurturing environment the past year, and where the owners Susan Miller and Rico Viray, and the partners Jennifer Matthews and Elizabeth Elfenbein, have been extremely supportive of this project. Jennifer and Elizabeth also have provided expert interviews for this book. In particular, many of the figures within this book were developed by CementBloc colleagues.

Additional thanks to TIBCO Software for permission to utilize screen captures from their Spotfire software as diagrams within this book.

I would also like to thank the staff at Gower Publications for approaching me with their interest in this book, and helping to format, publish, and promote this volume in the marketplace.

Finally, and most especially, I would like to thank my loving family for their support during this project. My father-in-law Max Snijders provided a most welcoming office environment. My parents Sondra and Oscar have been proudly supportive. My niece Melissa Haimowitz provided some early website prototype illustrations. My wife Barbara, my son Nathan, and my daughters Eva and Deborah have continually cheered me on and encouraged me to focus on the end goal.

Preface

In recent years, there have been dramatic changes in the pharmaceutical promotional landscape, affecting both consumers and healthcare professionals. One consequence of these dynamics is the need for pharmaceutical companies to plan new kinds of dialogue and relationships with their stakeholders. The evolution has been from mass-channel "push" marketing to two-way, multi-channel relationship marketing.

This book is intended as a practical overview and resource guide for the design and measurement of pharmaceutical relationship marketing programs. There are descriptions of each aspect of pharmaceutical relationship marketing (RM) design and measurement, including a running case study with follow-up exercises. The author has also conducted interviews with several pharmaceutical marketing industry experts, allowing each to speak on their specific specialties within pharmaceutical relationship marketing. This will enable readers to hear directly from senior practitioners, each having 15 years or more of working healthcare RM knowledge. We will cover both Consumer Relationship Marketing (CRM), aimed primarily at patients and caregivers, and Professional Relationship Marketing (PRM), aimed at physicians, nurses, office staff, and other healthcare professionals (HCPs).

For newcomers to healthcare marketing, this book can serve as a foundation and introduction that provides framework, details, and examples of both relationship marketing designs and associated measurement disciplines. The book will also be valuable to readers currently working in pharmaceutical marketing or sales and who may not have exposure to the particular disciplines of relationship marketing and direct response measurement and optimization. Even for the experienced practitioner, the author hopes this book can serve as a convenient reference that pulls together all of the program components and measurement frameworks within a single book. This book may also serve as a textbook within a university course in marketing, or a pharmaceutical business program.

A few important disclaimers are worth noting here in the Preface before the reader commences. The perspective taken in this book is primarily that of the branded drug manufacturer, because those are the companies that are most often commissioning and fielding CRM programs. However, this book is not taking a stand on treating medical conditions with branded drugs any more than generic drugs. Furthermore, throughout the sections on CRM, this book talks about motivating the patient to take actions. This is with the clear recognition that the decisions about writing prescriptions are made by licensed healthcare professionals. What follows logically is that this book does not recommend any medical diagnosis or treatment, nor does this book claim any medical expertise; a licensed healthcare professional should be sought for all medical decisions.

Periodically we describe details or illustrations of specific websites, data vendors, or software tools. However, neither the author nor this book explicitly endorses or recommends any particular vendor, manufacturer, or other healthcare-related suppliers.

Finally, it is worth noting that healthcare marketing is a very dynamic industry, particularly in the digital space. The perspectives given related to the healthcare industry and marketing trends reflect the latest thinking as of 2009 and 2010, when this book was written. In the years ahead some of those trends may evolve, especially related to communication channels like search, social media, and mobile technologies. Nevertheless, the principles of relationship marketing and how to measure success should remain stable over the years, even if the communication channels and the in-market channels evolve. For this reason, the author hopes this book will prove valuable for many years to come. In addition, to keep up with the latest trends, readers are invited to view the author's related blog at http://healthcarerm.blogspot.com/.

About the Cover Art

The book cover jacket was designed and fully developed by Mimia Johnson, our talented Art Director at The CementBloc. Aside from the striking, engaging appearance, there is much symbolism throughout the design.

The book title is rotated for effect, and embellished at ends with instantly recognizable, traditional medical symbols: caduceus, stethoscope, and ECG heartbeat data. The back cover foreground is a set of conversational blurbs, symbolizing the growing prominence of two-way dialogue and social networking within relationship marketing.

Finally, lurking behind is an array of multi-faceted, multi-channel elements of healthcare relationship marketing: stakeholders, technology, communications, and analytics. We will discuss all of these elements throughout the book, while detailing the dependencies and interrelationships. CementBloc founding partner Rico Viray is fond of saying that the tactics of healthcare communications are like individual stars across the sky, but that a truly integrated relationship marketing system is a constellation that ties these stars together. The author hopes the reader will find this book helpful in developing your own constellations, and navigating through the seas toward improved healthcare, just as ancient mariners did centuries ago.

Healthcare Trends and Relationship Marketing's Role

The Increasing Importance of Healthcare Marketing to Consumers

Within the past several years, an ever-larger share of US pharmaceutical marketing expenditure is focused on consumers and patients. According to Kantar Health media spending data, consumer pharmaceutical advertising rose by nearly 4 percent from 2008 to 2009, to a total of $4.8 billion, and that during a year when consumer advertisement spending across all industries decreased by 12.3 percent (Iskowitz March 2010). This rise in consumer spending is not only due to decreased spending on sales forces, but also because pharmaceutical companies are recognizing that patients are playing an ever-more active role in the management of their own health.

There are two primary factors for this more active health management by consumers:

1. Consumers have an *increased financial burden* in the cost of keeping healthy. Patients are now paying an ever-increasing share of pharmaceutical prescription costs in the form of deductibles, copays, or cash where they have no health insurance. As a result, patients are more interested than ever in the cost of medical treatments, and the value received for each expense.

2. Consumers in the digital age now have unprecedented access to information about wellness programs, diseases, treatments, and medications. Indeed, newly diagnosed or newly treating patients

have always had many questions about their health. Now these patients can find answers to their questions very quickly via the Internet, with or without a healthcare professional (HCP). Therefore, pharmaceutical companies have realized they must not only advertise one-way by pushing information out to consumers, instead, there must be a true two-way dialogue.

For many branded pharmaceutical manufacturers, this has significant and practical consequences. First, pharmaceutical companies have to provide credible, relevant sources of information that can help patients manage their health. Because patients are increasingly well-informed, that information must include a point of differentiation justifying why a patients should ask a doctor for the new drug. That point of differentiation may be an innovative mechanism of action, or a superior efficacy/safety profile. Alternatively, and in some cases additionally, there needs to be another type of *value exchange*. A few examples of value exchanges are additional information, support services, journals for charting progress, or reminders to take medication.

Second, the financial burden of pharmaceuticals means patients have to make difficult choices when thinking about beginning treatment. Note that an increasing percentage of all prescriptions filled in the USA are generic medications, 75 percent in 2009, according to an IMS Health Report. Because branded pharmaceutical drugs are more expensive, manufacturers sometimes offer financial assistance to patients, such as copay discount cards, helping them to pay for their medication in return for signing up to receive further condition or product information.

Focus of This Book

Information, support and incentives are the critical elements of the main topic of this book: relationship marketing (RM) programs. Let's define that topic, starting with consumers.

A consumer relationship marketing (CRM) program in pharmaceuticals is a series of information and incentives aimed at moving consumers along a pathway within a therapeutic category.

That pathway will be defined further in Chapter 2, but for now, think of that pathway as beginning as an undiagnosed consumer who is unaware of a particular therapeutic category, and ending as a patient regularly taking a particular medication within that category.

Note that in this book we will often refer to pharmaceuticals, but really the principles apply in broader terms, to include a wide range of health remedies. These include prescription drugs, over-the-counter medications, and nutritional products such as vitamins or infant formula.

Also noteworthy are the vast numbers of consumers that are not patients themselves, but are instead *caregivers* for others. They may be professional caregivers, such as nurses or home health aides, or they may simply be a friend or relative of a patient needing assistance (emotional or physical). Caregivers are especially widespread for chronic, degenerative diseases like cancer, AIDS, and neurological disorders.

Consumer Relationship Marketing in Pharmaceuticals versus Other Industries

Pharmaceutical CRM has similarities and differences to CRM in many other sectors such as financial services, airlines, and packaged goods. The main similarity is that CRM across industries is trying to persuade consumers to use a product, and to remain loyal to that product. Because of that similarity, much of the CRM design tactics and measurement tools in this book will be broadly applicable across many industries.

There are at least two primary factors making pharmaceutical CRM somewhat unique to other industries. The first is the heavily regulated environment. The US Food and Drug Administration (FDA) has specific regulations on pharmaceutical communications governed by its Division of Drug Marketing, Advertising, and Communications (DDMAC) which reviews consumer and professional promotion. Pharmaceutical manufacturers, responding to these tight regulations, have developed their own internal processes of medical/legal review. On an as-needed basis, typically once or twice per week, marketers, lawyers, and medical specialists meet to refine promotional materials so that they will meet FDA standards. We will not review the regulations in depth here, more details may be found at the DDMAC website (http://www.fda.gov/AboutFDA/CentersOffices/CDER/ucm090142.htm).

In order to ensure their literature is meeting FDA standards, marketers can train with organization such as the Center for Communication Compliance (http://www.communicationcompliance.com/go/Home). Most relevant to CRM are restrictions on product claims (must be clinically proven), comparisons to competitors (must be clinically proven as well), and consumer incentives (must be medically relevant and of modest value).

The second specific factor shaping pharmaceutical CRM is the fact that the consumer does not directly purchase the product. As illustrated in Figure 1.1, there are a host of other influences that shape whether a patient gets a particular prescription. Patients desiring a specific prescription must have a conversation with their physician—who is licensed to prescribe medications. Other HCPs in the office (nurses, office staff) may be influential, although they cannot prescribe. The physician then writes a prescription, which the patient then typically fills at a pharmacy. Pharmacists are influential for several reasons: not only do they give advice on taking medication, they also process the insurance transaction and communicate to patients the cost to be paid for their drugs.

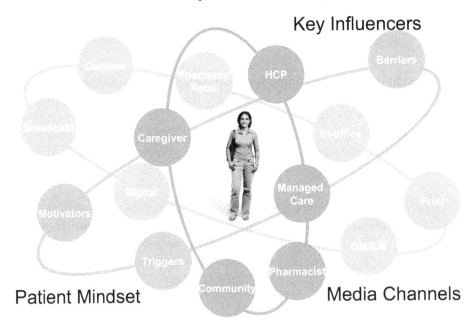

Figure 1.1   Healthcare influences upon consumers

Cost of medication is a critical issue in the US, and thus the *payer* is instrumental in determining whether a patient actually receives the medication prescribed. Payers may be a private insurance company, the Government (as in Medicare of Medicaid), or patients themselves, if they are paying in cash. Payers develop formularies (lists) of drugs approved for payment, and patients usually have to pay a copayment from their own pocket to supplement the insurance payment. For example, a three-tiered insurance benefit may be as follows for a 30-day supply of lipid-lowering cholesterol medications:

- patient pays $5 for generic medications;

- patient pays a $25 copay for a branded medication on the formulary;

- patient pays a $50 copay for a branded medication not on the formulary.

Such a payment structure may cause a patient to switch medications from the doctor-prescribed intended medication to a generic substitution, or even a branded substitution at a lower price.

Influences on Consumer Health Decisions

What factors determine whether a patient will take action to lower their cholesterol, to quit smoking, to treat their allergies, or to lose weight? Stagnation and inertia may be the simplest path. However, as illustrated in Figure 1.1, there are a range of influences upon consumers that can help them change the way they manage their personal healthcare.

1. The patient's mindset sets the baseline of how likely it is that they will take action. Moving the patient forward may require particular motivators, such as longevity, a better quality of life, or future family events the patient wishes to attend (for example, the weddings of their children). There may also be triggers that can stimulate action such as the death of a loved one, or a realization of increased risk. On the negative side, a patient may have barriers to action: inertia, a lack of urgency, or the high cost of medication. A person may also feel they cannot control their personal health outcomes.

2. Key influencers are outside sources that can spur the consumer to action. HCPs, including doctors and nurses, are well-positioned to

influence patients based on their training, experience, and personal contactHCPs can make direct recommendations including the prescription of medications. Another key influencer is a *caregiver*, especially for oncology patients, for children, or for the elderly. In these cases, the caregiver may be the one making decisions on medication and administering the doses. Other key influencers include the *pharmacist*, who fills the prescriptions and educates patients on alternative options, manages care insurance companies that maintain drug formularies and controls copay prices for patients. Finally, there is the broad social circle we call the *community* of the patient: this includes friends, family, and neighbors that share their experiences with similar diseases, and how they were treated. Within the past few years, this community has come to also include the electronic social network of a patient. This patient community warrants its own section later in this chapter.

3.   A third influencer is the broad set of media and communication channels that the patient consumes, as illustrated in Figure 1.1. Everywhere the patient goes, on every screen, there are continual messages about healthcare and pharmaceuticals. These media channels include:

- broadcast television and radio;

- digital media like banner ads, search engines, and healthcare portals;

- in-office materials at the doctor's office and retail pharmacy;

- printed advertising in popular magazines;

- outdoor publicity including billboards, health fairs, and even taxicabs;

- direct communications, via postal mail, email, and text messaging.

These advertisements, communications, and targeted medical content help shape the consumer's information base and options about therapeutic categories and particular medications.

The Rise of Online Social Networks as a Consumer influence

One influence that has risen in prominence recently is the Internet-based social network. Beyond the basics of looking up conditions and medications, health information seekers are increasingly going online in search of inspiration to help them deal with specific health challenges that they or their family members face. New forms of social computing are emerging for healthcare; from expert health blogs that turn medical information into conversation to social networks that inspire with personal stories. Indeed, consumers are increasingly turning to the Internet for healthcare answers, to seek out clinical expertise from HCPs, and to read personal stories from other patients. For example:

- A social network called Daily strength (www.dailystrength.org), provides patient-to-patient support groups, including a forum where patients can actually provide informal feedback on the efficacy of prescription (Rx) medications.

- PatientsLikeMe (www.patientslikeme.com) is a patient social media site covering a wide range of therapeutic classes, where patients enter basic diagnosis and demographic information, and exchange case histories and experiences.

The use of social media is not limited to a younger demographic, nor is it specific to any particular therapeutic categories; the phenomenon is widespread. In a recent Forrester Research technology adoption survey (Forester 2006), it was found that 15 to 30 percent of consumers used social media for health issues, across a wide range of therapeutic categories including migraines, depression, high cholesterol, arthritis, weight loss, and oncology. All of these conditions have a median patient age of 40 to 60. Those percentages have been increasing in recent years.

Industry Expert Perspective

To gain perspective on the impact and future place of CRM within the healthcare environment, we have turned to Becky Chidester, an expert in the field. Becky is the President of Wunderman World Health's global health unit. Wunderman has been one of the world's leading direct marketing firms since 1958 and is a member of the WPP company. Previously, Becky was President of Wunderman's New York office and RTC Relationship Marketing in Washington, DC. In both agencies, and for nearly two decades, Becky has played an integral leadership role in developing innovative healthcare communications to consumers in the US. Below are excerpts from an interview with Becky on the role of CRM in pharmaceuticals, and what the future may hold.

Haimowitz: What is the role of CRM within the overall pharmaceutical consumer advertising mix?

Chidester: The role of CRM will continue to grow in importance, not only within the advertising and marketing mix, but also in the way that pharmaceutical firms have to approach their business. Pharmaceutical companies have to appreciate the need to be relevant, and to meet individual consumers' needs, from a healthcare perspective. There is an important opportunity for pharmaceutical companies to have a conversation with consumers and meet their relevant healthcare needs. It transforms the way companies have approached the patients: from pushing them into the doctor's office, to addressing what the patients are really trying to solve: such as diagnosis, and what medicines are right for them. RM will be the catalyst for that transformation because of its heritage of creating dialogues with consumers.

Haimowitz: What has changed in the pharmaceutical industry to precipitate this transformation?

Chidester: What has changed in the past ten years is that the patient's time with HCPs is more limited. Thanks to technology, consumers now have the ability to have their questions and needs answered by going online or using their mobile phones to access information. The Internet has satisfied that need for dialogue that patients have as well. Thanks to the healthcare debate (during the Obama administration) serving as a backdrop; commentary on healthcare and cost were thrust on to the front pages of newspapers and magazines. Therefore, consumers are more aware of medical treatment options, insurance options, even fraud and abuse practices. The result is consumers need to be more active in managing their situation, which also opens the door for an increasing role for CRM.

Haimowitz: What are the unique challenges that the pharmaceutical industry faces in conducting CRM?

Chidester: There is one significant challenge: a company can never have a transactional relationship with consumers, because they can never know precisely what people are engaged in after they become patients and follow through with their healthcare. The best companies can do is provide consumers with tailored content, based on information that consumers are willing to communicate to a company, or what can be inferred from website behaviors. However, a company generally is left uncertain as to whether the consumer really took the action. (This is due both to HIPAA regulations as well as occasional absence of data.) For example, persistence or compliance may generally improve in a CRM program, but for individual patients in an adherence program, this change is unknown unless that patient directly communicates with you about his or her behavior. And in regards to adherence, the window to influence compliance and persistence is so short, in most categories the time period is the first three months of taking the product! This is another reason that CRM is a challenge in pharmaceuticals.

Haimowitz: How rapidly is the pharmaceutical industry adopting new media channels in CRM, such as mobile and social networks?

Chidester: The pharmaceutical industry is very nervous and cautious about adopting some of these channels because of industry requirements. After all, sensitive medical content can be communicated. These channels are not going away and the industry must look for ways to participate in social networks and patient communities. The notion of people wanting to communicate and share their experiences will not go away. The number of conversations is only going to increase. More and more people are balancing how they take information from experts versus the experience of others.

My experience has shown me how personal healthcare is to consumers. Despite the science (expressed in populations and cohorts), people still feel their medical experience is unique because it's based on their heritage, their lifestyle, and how they want to be treated. Patients interpret general information in terms of what is right for them, whether there are side effects or how other patients have been treated with medications. The ultimate need for consumers is to find the "right solution for me," and they will keep seeking information from others, expert or otherwise. The onus is on the healthcare community to continue to evolve.

Haimowitz: As we are now in 2010 and a new decade, how will pharmaceutical CRM continue to change versus programs of the last 20 years?

Chidester: The answer lies primarily in connections and flow of information between constituents: consumers, HCPs, payers, and manufacturers. Although pharmaceutical companies understand the convergence between all of these constituents, it is hard to find companies that are paying that off. How do you connect all of these into a larger conversation that will ultimately benefit the patients? This depends partly on what happens in the US with healthcare reform: some aspects will promote better healthcare integration, efficiencies, and communications. The future is not specifically about CRM or new media. It's about the connections between patients, HCPs, payers and manufacturer, to insure better results.

Influences for Healthcare Professionals

Just as we have described the many influences on consumers, there are similarly a range of influences on HCPs, as they consider a prescribing a pharmaceutical product. These influences are depicted in Figure 1.2.

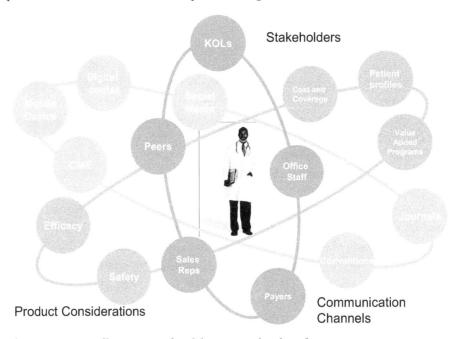

Figure 1.2   Influences on healthcare professionals

One dimension of influence is the *product considerations*. These include the efficacy and safety profiles of the drug, as well as the clinical profiles of patients within a doctor's practice. Another product consideration is the cost of medication, and the managed care formulary coverage. Finally, the HCP also looks to value-added programs that may come along with a product. Examples of these programs can be:

- patient education materials that manage their expectations;

- patient journals and diaries that help them chart their progress while on medication. These are frequent in categories like smoking cessation, weight loss, and migraine management. See Loftus (2009) for both paper and personal digital assistant (PDA) solutions for migraine patients;

- extended professional care resources for patients to call (or text chat) with any questions about the pharmaceutical product;

- administrative resources to office staff for handling payer issues like prior authorizations or step edits.

Another dimension of influence on HCPs is stakeholders. Doctors receive education about drugs and medical devices from sales representatives of the manufacturers. They also hear about new medications from other professional peers in their community, and key opinion leaders (KOLs) who are typically specialists that have been early adopters, or participants in clinical trials for that product. Payers are clearly a stakeholder that HCPs must pay attention to as they supply reimbursement and may even keep scorecards related to how adherent a physician's prescribing is to the approved formulary. Finally, the office staff is a key stakeholder within a physician practice; doctors need to think about training their staff and easing their administrative burden.

Yet another influence set on HCPs are the communication channels where they receive their information. Traditionally, in addition to the sales force, physicians receive product-related information through conventions, medical journals, and continuing medical education. More recently, increasing numbers of professionals are regularly using mobile devices such as Epocrates, which distributes DocAlerts with information on new drugs and medical devices. There has also been a rise in the number and utilization of professional social media such as:

- Sermo (www.sermo.com);

- Medscape (www.medscape.com); and

- Ozmosis (www.ozmosis.com).

On these professional social media sites, physicians share their impressions of new medications, and may discuss anonymous patient cases to get professional opinions. Finally, physicians and other professionals often get product information via an ever-expanding array of digital content, which can be found on pharmaceutical-branded websites, professional association portals, newswires, or professional blogs. Some of these Internet locations may offer electronic details (e-details), or clinical product presentations presented in video and slide presentation format. These e-details can be wholly self-service, or they can be guided by telephone representative support.

The Changing Healthcare Professional Promotional Landscape

In recent years, there has been significant upheaval in pharmaceutical promotion to HCPs. For decades, manufacturers have employed thousands of door-to-door sales representatives to educate physicians, nurses, and office staff about new medications and related health programs. Within recent years, the size of these sales forces has been gradually shrinking. The reductions stem from the economic forces facing pharmaceutical companies, as well as from doctor's having decreased time and willingness to meet with sales reps. Concurrently, increasing numbers of HCPs are spending time on the Internet and on mobile devices, seeking information on medical treatments as well as dialogue and advice from peer-to-peer communities.

The reach of pharmaceutical sales representatives in professional promotion has changed dramatically. Some recent data illustrate this point (SK&A 2010). According to SK&A, by December 2009, 22.9 percent of MDs refused to see sales representatives, and a total of 49.6 percent require or prefer an appointment to be seen. Consequently, in the pharmaceutical industry, the volume of sales representatives is declining, down by 10 percent since 2007 and expected to drop by another 18 percent by 2012, as documented by ZS Associates in 2009 and reported in the Wall Street Journal Blog March 23, 2009.

Concurrently there is a rise in physician use of the Internet. According to SDI, 53 percent of all sales details in 2007 were self-led virtual details (Giegerich 2010). Manhattan Research has been tracking the trends in "ePharma" physicians, which means they use the Internet and other technologies to interact with drug and biotech companies. The percentage of such ePharma physicians has risen from 64 percent in 2004 to 87 percent in 2009 (Vecchione 2009).

Furthermore, the very nature of physician prescribing is evolving to become more digital. Martin (2010) notes that physicians are increasingly turning to e-prescribing software on computer laptops, turning away from paper-based prescriptions with hard to read handwriting, and with the potential for rejection by payers due to prescribed products not being on a patient formulary. According to online network vendor Surescripts LLC, the number of e-prescriptions nearly tripled from 68 million in 2008 to 191 million in 2009, and now represents about 12 percent of the 1.63 billion new prescriptions in the USA, excluding refills. With e-prescribing, medications and their proper doses are selected from lists, and their status automatically checked against patient insurer formularies. This digital trend is not just a fad; e-prescribing has been shown to reduce medical practice errors: according to a Cornell Medical Center-based study of 12 community-based medical practices (Kaushal et al. 2010), practices using e-prescribing dramatically cut error rates (wrong medication or dosages) from 42.5 percent to 6.6 percent on average, compared to a matched control group of medical practices using paper prescriptions rising from 37 percent to 38 percent.

In light of these dynamics, over the past few years pharmaceutical companies have recognized they need to develop multifaceted professional promotional systems. These systems must consist in part of efficient automated solutions for reaching HCPs and to increase accountability, measurement, and optimization.

A sample of these solutions includes:

- tablet PCs that display visual aids electronically and interactively, and capture data on the messaging sequence presented;

- self-service website portals where HCPs can view product information or download patient educational materials;

- guided video e-details with call center support (for example, Aptilon) where doctors see messaging on their schedule;

- mobile information delivery on Epocrates and QuantiaMD;

- professional communities where physicians can discuss clinical cases, new medications, and practice management issues.

These changes add up to a new thinking in HCP marketing, parallel in many ways to consumer marketing. Pharmaceutical companies are now implementing dialogue-based, multi-channel, electronic communication platforms for HCPs. We will refer to these platforms as professional relationship marketing (PRM). Underlying the new, shifting nature of the professional is a varied and evolving nomenclature. Different pharmaceutical companies have developed a variety of other phrases and acronyms for these professional promotion programs:

- Professional relationship marketing (PRM)

- Non-personal promotion (NPP)

- Multi-channel marketing (MCM)

- Closed loop marketing (CLM)

- Closed loop promotion (CLP).

The "closed loop" phrases illustrate another critical component: the desire to continually measure, learn, and improve. Companies want to measure patterns of how doctors, nurses, and other HCPs interact with the digital channels, and then use those patterns to:

- inform the sales representatives for their next face to-face calls;

- dynamically adjust and personalize website portals, emails, and mobile tactics; and

- revise overall marketing strategy based on what messages have either succeeded or failed previously.

Who This Book is For

This book will describe how pharmaceutical companies and their strategic partners can develop RM programs for both consumers and HCPs. It will also describe how to measure such programs for effectiveness against business goals, and continually improve.

The author has written this book as a practical overview and resource guide for people fielding RM programs. For newcomers to healthcare marketing, this book can serve as a foundation and introduction that provides a framework, details, and examples of both RM designs and associated measurement disciplines. Indeed, as mentioned earlier, much of what is presented here will apply not only in healthcare but also to other industries. Some readers who are already working in pharmaceutical marketing or sales may not have exposure to the particular disciplines of RM and direct response measurement and optimization. Even for the experienced practitioner, the author hopes this book can serve as a convenient reference that pulls together all of the program components and measurement frameworks within a single book.

This book may also serve as a textbook within a university advanced course in marketing, or a pharmaceutical business program. With this in mind, we have included a case study of a hypothetical (yet realistic) pharmaceutical brand, roughly one year after its launch. The case study is introduced in Chapter 2 and a series of exercises on that case study appear in later chapters. Readers within a classroom setting may assign these exercises as homework. Individual readers, of course, may work through these examples on their own, or simply read through the case study, questions, and solutions. The answers are outlined as an Appendix at the end of the book.

There was some debate during the writing of this book as to whether to combine or to separate the treatment of RM of consumers from RM to HCPs. Ultimately, the choice was made to write with an integrated approach, and to interleave CRM and PRM. While the author recognizes that some pharmaceutical marketers or healthcare agencies may focus predominantly on consumers only, or on professionals only, these two stakeholders are by nature intertwined in medical treatment. Furthermore, when one speaks of strategy or measurement for consumers, there are many similarities in the technical approach, regardless of whether one is marketing to consumers or to HCPs. It is hoped that this interleaving makes the book more enjoyable and less disjointed.

In a similar vein, the author also realizes that various companies, whether manufacturer, consultancy, data supplier, or communications agency, have departments and roles divided by technical specialty. Examples of such technical specialties are: market research, media, web analytics, statistical modeling, or campaign operations. Readers falling into one of these specialties may ask, "Which sections of this book are best for me to read?" The short answer to that question would be, "All of them," as we have written this book with an integrated approach based on the project lifecycle, and we feel that all specilialists have a role throughout RM development. However, in an attempt to provide guidance to such a question, we have mapped out Figure 1.3. This chart shows, for each role, which are the most salient chapters to be read, to understand how that specialist contributes to the healthcare RM process. Note that we recommend people in each role to read most of the chapters, and we advise everyone to read the chapter following this one, on the fundamentals of RM.

Professional Role	Fundamentals	Discovery	Strategy	Analytics Planning	Execution	Measurement	Optimization
Strategy/ Market Research	√	√	√	√		√	
Media	√	√	√			√	√
Operations/ Campaign Management	√	√		√	√	√	√
Web analytics	√	√		√	√	√	√
Statistical Modeler	√			√	√	√	

Figure 1.3　　Book focus areas by job specialty

Primarily, this book describes programs' healthcare trends and RM programs based in the US. The techniques we describe for planning, measurement, and optimization should apply equally well to other countries. Furthermore, the healthcare environment in other countries outside the US may be even more dynamic. One interesting recent study conducted by Kantar Health (Arnold, March 2010) has actually shown that European physicians and consumers are "more receptive to the use of social media for health information than are their American counterparts." In particular:

- 67 percent of European consumers trust information they find in social-media venues, compared to 45 percent of American consumers;

- 52 percent of European physicians said healthcare professionals should participate in discussions within patient forums and social networks. This compares to only 41 percent of US physicians.

Author's Notes on Technical Depth

One distinction of RM (and its critical component direct marketing), over other types of marketing decision making, is the ability to quantify and measure progress against business objectives. Indeed, the past two decades have seen increasing acknowledgement that quantitative methods are critical to driving business decision making. This includes the six sigma statistical revolution popularized early on by Motorola and General Electric (Eckes 2001), to leveraging analytics in marketing as a competitive threat (Davenport and Harris 2007). Therefore, this book will present a treatment of RM rooted in quantitative principles and appropriate data sources.

That said, as the author, I have tried to create, in the same volume, a readable overview of pharmaceutical RM, as well as a technical resource for the practitioner. To achieve both of these goals, I have had to make choices as to how deeply to approach certain technical topics. Generally speaking, I have tried to introduce the formal, technical foundations of many marketing concepts in a way that most readers can understand and appreciate. I have named particular techniques within the marketing contexts in which they are used.

However, I have stopped short of reproducing full derivations of formulas and algorithms, choosing instead to refer the reader to standard textbooks for in-depth treatments. For example, in the section on segmentation within Chapter 4, concepts like principal components analysis and clustering are introduced as foundational, but the reader is referred to excellent textbooks on multivariate analysis like Dillon and Goldstein (1984) and Duda, Hart and Stork (2001). Similarly, while I have given a basic overview of media planning and media purchase schedules for CRM, I view as outside the scope of this book any detailed discussions of advertising media purchasing or consumption tracking, instead referring the reader to Baron and Sissors (2010).

As another way of providing expertise in this book, I have asked several colleagues to provide interviews on their specific specialties within pharmaceutical RM. This will enable readers to hear directly from senior practitioners, each having 15 to 20 years of working CRM knowledge. These experts are also well positioned to preview future industry trends in pharmaceutical marketing communications. I hope I have achieved the desired product of a valuable overview, textbook, and reference for all.

Foundations of Relationship Marketing

In this chapter we lay the foundations of consumer relationship marketing (CRM), both generally, and specifically as they apply to pharmaceuticals. The concepts and specific terminology in this chapter will be used often throughout the rest of the book. We also describe the elements of professional relationship marketing (PRM) as well.

The Patient Journey

The *patient journey* is the actual set of interactions that a consumer experiences on the way to moving across the treatment spectrum. It includes media consumed across all channels and interactions with various personal influencers including healthcare professionals (HCPs) of different specialties. Consumers move through a series of stages in their relationship with a branded medication. These stages are illustrated in Figure 2.1.

In the earliest stages, a consumer is *pre-diagnosed*, and is unaware they have a particular condition or a disease. The consumer may have symptoms and not understand what is causing them. Such an example is the chronic widespread pain experienced in fibromyalgia. Alternatively, the patient may have an asymptomatic condition and not even know there is a problem. Examples of this type of condition are hypertension and hyperlipidemia.

The next stage of the patient journey is *diagnosis*, where patients seek attention from a HCP, usually a doctor, and are informed they have a particular condition or disease. The following stage is *treatment,* where the doctor writes a prescription for a medication, and patients fill the prescription at the pharmacy.

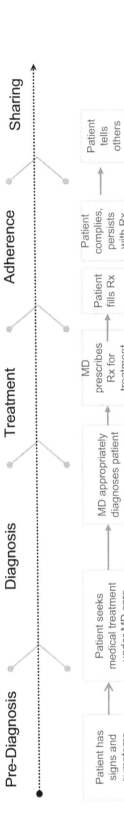

Figure 2.1   The patient journey

The patient will require product information on what to expect and is likely to follow up with the physician or pharmacy if there are side effects.

Note we describe the diagnosis and treatment stages specifically for traditional "Western" medicine where a medical doctor writes a prescription medication. Certainly, there are alternative pathways where a patient may visit seek "alternative therapy" like acupuncture or herbal remedies. A patient may also self-medicate with over-the-counter products, prevalent in the allergy, pain, and respiratory categories. These are viable patient journeys, which can either complement or compete with prescriptions for the patient market share. However, for the rest of this book, we will focus primarily on patient journeys involving prescription medications.

After treatment with a prescription, the next phase is patient *adherence*, meaning continuity on the medication over an extended period of time. Actually, adherence consists of two components:

- *Compliance*, meaning the patient is taking the medication as directed by the prescriber: with the right dosage and daily frequency.

- *Persistence*, meaning the patient is taking the medication over as long a time period as needed.

Lack of medication adherence is one of the major challenges to pharmaceutical companies. According to a recent consumer survey conducted by the National Community Pharmacists Association (2007), adherence challenges take on many forms:

- 49 percent of those polled said they had forgotten to take a prescribed medication;

- 31 percent of consumers polled did not fill an Rx they were given;

- 29 percent of polled consumers stopped taking a medication before the supply ran out; and

- 24 percent of patients had taken less than their recommended dosage.

A recent report by the National Council on Patient Information and Education (2006) noted that "lack of medication adherence leads to unnecessary disease progression, disease complications, reduced functional abilities, a lower quality of life, and even premature death." In the US "poor adherence has been estimated to cost approximately $177 billion annually in total direct and indirect healthcare costs."

The final phase to describe applies to those patients who are very satisfied with their therapy, and are *sharing* their experiences. They may either supply a testimonial to the pharmaceutical company, using a feature like "tell your story" or they may communicate to their friends, in person, or via their social network on the Internet.

The nature of patient journeys differs across therapeutic categories and across patient segments. For some indications, the patient journey is quite direct and focuses on a single HCP. A person with a mild respiratory infection visits a primary care physician (PCP), who usually selects the appropriate antibiotic based on the diagnosis and the drug's indication. The pharmacy will fill the antibiotic or a generic equivalent. There may or may not be a follow-up between patient and physician later to check if the infection persists. By contrast, in oncology, multiple specialists and medications are often involved over time.

How Consumer Relationship Marketing Affects the Patient Journey

A CRM program in pharmaceuticals is aimed at moving patients along a journey from undiagnosed and untreated, to taking therapy, and to remaining adherent on that therapy. Understanding patient journeys within a therapeutic category is the foundation of developing impactful CRM programs. An effective CRM program will accelerate the movement of a consumer along the patient journey, from left to right. As illustrated in Figure 2.2, different phases of CRM are focused on achieving this goal at different stages of the journey.

ACQUISITION

The *acquisition* phase of relationship marketing (RM) is to get patients closer to proper diagnosis. This phase encourages patients to seek more information, from any or all of a combination of sources:

- their HCPs;

Pre-Diagnosis   Diagnosis   Treatment   Adherence   Sharing

Acquisition   Conversion   Retention   Advocacy

- Spread condition awareness
- Grow a consumer database
- Preliminary segmentation.

- Enable patient doctor conversation
- Encourage patient Rx trial

- Manage patient expectations
- Tracking journals, diaries
- Offer support services

- Enable patient feedback
- Build, leverage communities

Figure 2.2   Consumer relationship marketing and the patient journey

- an information resource like a website; or

- registering to receive additional information by direct mail (DM) or email (EM).

If a registration vehicle is included, then a pharmaceutical company can build a consumer database with contact information, so that they can have an ongoing dialogue of communications with these consumers. The registration form will include contact information, an opt-in clause giving permission for further contact, and a series of survey questions aimed at finding out more about the consumer. The registration survey questions can enable a preliminary segmentation of those consumers who sign up, and that segmentation can be used for customized communication tactics by segment. We will have more to say on registration design for acquisition later in this book.

Note that acquisition campaigns fall into two categories:

- *Branded acquisition campaigns* encourage consumers to find out more about a specific medication by name.

- *Unbranded acquisition campaigns* encourage consumers to learn about a general category of disease.

The choice of whether to use branded versus unbranded acquisition campaigns is based primarily on the competitive marketplace conditions. If a company's drug is first or second to market within a new therapeutic category, then unbranded acquisition is advisable. The unbranded campaign would educate the marketplace about the condition, and encourage consumers to find out more information. Eventually, branded tactics can follow that will insure patients are also educated about the new brand. However, if the therapeutic category is highly competitive with many branded and even generic entrants, then a branded acquisition campaign is more advisable, distinguishing the new product from the competitors, and encouraging patients to ask for it by name when seeing their doctor.

CONVERSION

The next phase of CRM is called *conversion*, also shown in Figure 2.2. While the acquisition phase helps to drive patients into the doctor's office and get diagnosed, the conversion phase communications help insure that patients are treated with a particular medication. Conversion tactics fall within these categories:

- *Facilitating the patient-doctor dialogue* by providing materials for patients to bring to the doctor's office. These include checklists, in-office surveys, and other tools to encourage the physician to make a particular diagnosis and write a certain therapy. This has proved especially successful in categories where patients may be uncomfortable discussing their condition like depression and erectile dysfunction, or where conditions are often misdiagnosed like pain categories. A more recent conversion tactic is Phreesia, a waiting room sign-in tablet where patients can receive education or take surveys specific to their medical complaints.

- *Encourage patient trial* by lowering the barriers to trial and providing incentives. Example tactics accomplishing this include starter kits with product samples and valuable information on what to expect with the new medication. Another example is financial incentives like copay discount cards that decrease the out-of-pocket costs to a patient, especially for the first prescription.

RETENTION

The *retention* phase of CRM is deployed to encourage patient adherence. Recall from earlier that adherence is both compliance (taking medication as indicated) and persistence (taking medication over time). Retention tactics for pharmaceuticals include:

- Brochures and websites that manage patient expectations about how to take their medications and how they may feel after starting therapy.

- Avenues for dialogue with the patient, whether that be through a telephone call center, through specialized websites, or through a continual stream of DM or EM communications.

- Methods for charting progress on improvement of symptoms, like diaries, journals, and symptom relief checklists. This enables a patient to continually see progress over time, and therefore stay motivated to continue taking medication.

ADVOCACY

As noted in Chapter 1, patients are frequently turning toward the Internet to seek medical advice, and are also sharing their medical experiences online. When a patient has a positive experience with a branded pharmaceutical, they may indeed wish to communicate outward, so that other patients can achieve the same health benefits. Pharmaceutical companies can enable this by establishing an *advocacy* component to their consumer CRM program. In other industries, advocacy programs are sometimes called "viral marketing," or even "member get a member."

Examples of pharmaceutical CRM advocacy tactics are:

- Direct feedback requests from patients, called "tell us your story," where patients can reply to the drug manufacturer about health improvements. The responses are reviewed, and some are placed on the product website or other branded communications.

- Forwarding of web pages or other content directly to other consumers, sometimes called "tell a friend." This tactic is based on the reality that patients with common disorders can be a close-knit community, and so a successfully treated patient will actually know others who may also benefit.

- Building or leveraging online communities. In many therapeutic categories, there are already a plethora of online social networks and chat rooms where patients are sharing experiences. A new, successful branded medication may inevitably become a part of that dialogue, and the pharmaceutical manufacturer would do well to participate. Where those online communities are not yet established, they can be created through an unbranded healthcare partnership.

Components of the Consumer Relationship Marketing Program

We now step through the components and interconnected design of a CRM program, as illustrated in Figure 2.3. The complexity is illustrated via the wide array of connected modules. We shall explain each of these from left to right, starting with the consumer.

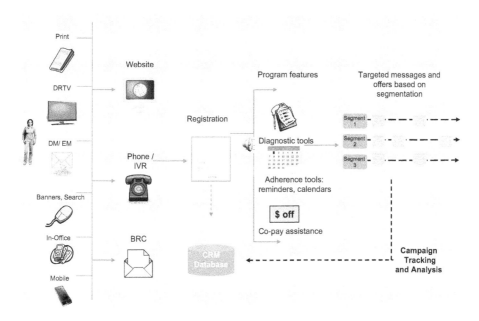

Figure 2.3   **Consumer relationship marketing overview**

PROMOTIONAL CHANNELS

A consumer (who may be a patient or caregiver) interacts with a CRM program via several promotional channels, which are usually selected in a targeted approach to match the media consumption habits of that consumer. These can include one or more of:

- Print, including magazines and newspapers, which are usually selected for campaign targets based on a combination of geographic, demographic, and perceived interests.

- Television, (in particular direct response television, or DRTV), that can be similarly targeted by demographic background, or perceived behavioral interests.

- DM and EM, which can be either purchased from lists, or based on an already existing RM database.

- Banner advertising, which are usually placed in online media outlets targeted either by demographics or specific health content.

- Search engines, where consumers are seeking specific information regarding a health condition, disease, treatment, or a particular pharmaceutical product. What is interesting about search engines is their active nature; some marketers say that an Internet search is an "expression of intent," and therefore, consumers are more genuinely interested in search engine results than banner advertisements or other promotional vehicles. We shall discuss this more in our measurement sections. At the time of writing this book, the leading search engines in the US included Google, Yahoo, Bing, Ask, and AOL.

- In office materials, usually found in the waiting room of doctor's office and clinics.

- Mobile phone text messages, which though more innovative, may be a similar promotional mechanism to email, usually with a faster response and shorter character limits on messages.

RESPONSE VEHICLES AND REGISTRATION

There are three traditional vehicles by which a consumer can respond to a CRM program:

- *Website*: a consumer either types in the URL, or clicks through from an electronic promotion to visit a website. When clicking through, usually the destination is not the home page of the website, but rather a "landing page" that describes offers and features of the RM program and encourages registration.

- *Telephone*: when a phone number (usually toll-free) is supplied with a CRM promotional ad, a consumer calling that number may either speak to a person, often called a live agent, or interact with a menu-driven interactive voice response system (IVR).

- Business reply cards are printed within magazines, in-office materials, and DM pieces. The consumer handwrites contact information and checks boxes for any permissions.

The registration process typically has three critical components:

1. A form asking for contact information, whether it be postal address, email address, or mobile number.

2. A survey questionnaire that asks the consumer some (typically optional) questions on demographics and health-related questions appropriate to the therapeutic category.

3. Opt-in permission, usually as a check box, where the consumer gives permission to be contacted in the future by the pharmaceutical company.

THE CONSUMER RELATIONSHIP MARKETING DATABASE

Once registered, the patient's contact information and survey responses are entered into a CRM database that is Health Insurance Portability and Accountability Act (HIPAA) compliant. The consumer responses from each acquisition channel are collected on a regular basis and sent to a centralized CRM database, which is the information hub of all CRM activity. All relevant information regarding registered consumers and their interactions with the RM program is stored in this database. For this reason, it is critical that the CRM database be HIPAA compliant, and protects any personally identifiable medical information.

The survey responses provided by the consumer at the point of registration are also stored in the database and are analyzed to help assign this member into one of several segments. We will provide more details as to the components of this CRM database in a later chapter.

CONSUMER RELATIONSHIP MARKETING PROGRAM TOOLS

Members of a CRM program have access to a variety of offerings and tools which fall into these categories:

• Diagnostic tools, aimed particularly at consumers who are not yet diagnosed with a particular condition. Examples of these are *screening questionnaires* that patients complete to determine whether they might have a particular condition. Closely associated with these are *discussion guides* for patients to take to their doctors, to aid a discussion that may lead to a diagnosis, or even treatment.

• Adherence tools, aimed at patients who are on a particular medication, with the aim of keeping that patient compliant (taking as directed) and persistent (taking for extended periods of time as needed). Examples of these are journals, diaries, and reminder systems.

- Copay assistance cards, which are used to offset (partially or fully) the cost of a copayment that patients must pay the managed care company. It can also partially offset the cost for patients who pay cash for a medication. An interesting recent study by the Amundsen Group using Wolters Kluwer data (Tenaglia and Meister 2010) demonstrated that increased copays are associated with lower drug adherence and increased "reversals" by patients asking pharmacists not to fill the medication. Therefore, not surprisingly, copay assistance programs have become increasingly common to encourage trials of new branded medications in crowded therapeutic categories.

FOLLOW-UP COMMUNICATIONS

All CRM members that have registered in the database and opted-in for further ongoing communications are then sent information as illustrated in Figure 2.3. These are governed by a set of *business rules* broken down by segments. For example, patients who are diagnosed but not receiving medication will typically be sent different types of communications to patients who are already taking the particular drug which is the focus of the CRM program. This book will delve much further into customer segmentation and business rules for communication in later chapters.

In the early days of pharmaceutical CRM, such as the 1990s and early 2000s, CRM program communications were primarily "one-way" and paper-based. Materials were mailed by post from the manufacturer to consumers or patients, and there were rarely opportunities for that consumer to respond. More recently, these programs are increasingly digital, based on emails and a website portal, and they solicit feedback responses and brief surveys. Another feature, still more prevalent in over-the-counter health products, are community offerings where multiple consumers can chat and answer each other's questions.

CAMPAIGN TRACKING AND ANALYSIS

An integral part of CRM programs is the ability to track performance and make continual improvements. As the campaign proceeds, data is gathered by acquisition source and by each segment to understand the member base and to measure program effectiveness.

Campaign tracking includes:

- response rates and cost efficiencies of promotional media;

- monitoring of CRM membership levels and growth;

- engagement in program communications; and

- ultimately, prescription and sales impact of CRM membership over a matched control group.

We will go into greater depth on CRM campaign measurement in later chapters of this book.

The Physician Journey

Now that we have enumerated the patient journey and the components of a CRM program, we will go through a similar treatment for HCPs. Our emphasis is on physicians, but most of this development is applicable to other professionals such as nurses or educators. The primary distinction of physicians is that they prescribe medication, which is one of the critical decision points of professional relationship marketing (PRM). Note that this journey is also applicable to other healthcare products besides medications, such as diabetes test strips or medical devices.

The physician journey, as it relates to a particular medication or healthcare product, is illustrated in Figure 2.4. A similar journey exists for other healthcare products like medical devices, nutritionals, aesthetics, and so on. Listed below each phase of the journey are objectives for PRM.

The first two phases demonstrate that RM plays a role even before actual product usage. At the leftmost part of the journey is pre-awareness, the doctor is unaware of the medication, and PRM needs to introduce the product and its profile to the physicians. During the next phase, the doctor is aware of the medication, but has not yet actually prescribed it. For this phase, the goals of PRM are to encourage product trial by engaging the physician in dialogue

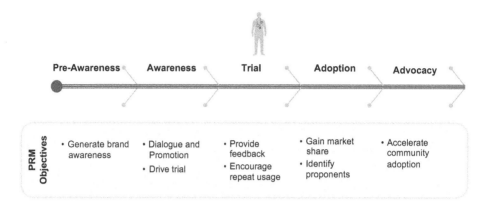

Figure 2.4   The healthcare professional journey

and promotional activities, whether via sales representatives, or non-personal promotion (NPP). This dialogue should be geared toward removing any remaining barriers to prescribe. As mentioned in Chapter 1, those barriers may include: cost of medication, administrative process in filling the prescription, novelty of a drug or product, or lack of proven in-market experience. These can be addressed with effective program services, and by making the physician part of a community, some of whose members have already prescribed.

The next three phases are those where a physician is actually prescribing the medication. There is the *trial* phase, where the physician has written at least one prescription for the product. During this phase, the goal of RM should be to encourage repeat usage. One way of accomplishing this is to provide feedback to the physician about early patient experience. The following phase is the *adoption* phase, where the doctor is regularly prescribing the medication. During this phase, RM can aim to increase product market share by reinforcing the physician's prescribing decision based on additional product information that may not have been shared to this point. PRM can also aim to identify physicians who may become proponents. Indeed, the final stage of the journey in Figure 2.4 is *advocacy,* where physicians share their experiences with other peers. A PRM program can facilitate this sharing with community features, and thereby accelerate product adoption amongst a broader range of physicians.

Components of a Professional Relationship Marketing Program

We have spoken about the objectives of RM throughout the professional journey. Now let's step through the components of a PRM system that aims to achieve those objectives. A typical healthcare PRM program is illustrated in Figure 2.5. There are many similarities with the CRM programs described earlier in this chapter.

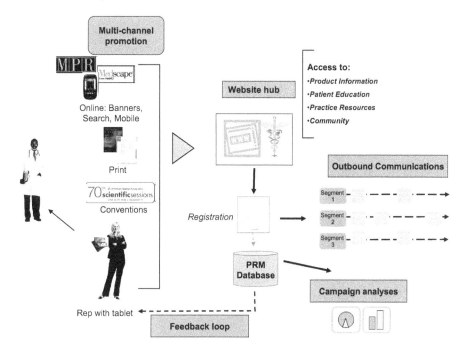

Figure 2.5   Professional relationship marketing system

Let's begin in the center of Figure 2.5 where there is typically a website that is the hub, or the gateway, for the PRM system. It is here that HCPs can receive a broad array of information, which we will break into four categories:

1.   *Product information:* these are descriptions of the products sold by the manufacturer that has developed the PRM system. There may be one product, or a portfolio of multiple related products. Examples of product information are:

      •   attributes, such as efficacy and safety profiles;

      •   instructions for dosing and administration to patients;

      •   information on related clinical trials.

Note each of these may be delivered in static documents, or as videos. One example of video may be a Key Opinion Leader (KOL) physician presenting clinical trial results for the product or the related category. Another is an e-detail with teleconference phone support.

2. *Patient education:* even though the content is patient focused, it is valuable within a PRM program because the HCP desires the right information to keep their patients healthy. A physician may wish to package up patient-oriented information content into a newsletter to be handed to appropriate patients, all branded with that doctor's name and office practice details. With this context in mind, patient education within a PRM program can take these forms:

    •   training on administration or dosage of specific products, especially relevant for medical devices. Related is information on what patients should expect as they use this product;

    •   alternatively, the patient education may be more about more general healthy lifestyle management. Topics for this may include smoking cessation, diet, exercise, or stress reduction;

    •   diagnostic screening tools;

    •   charting tools such as journals and diaries;

    •   information on patient copay assistance programs.

3. *Practice resources:* note that many HCPs are not only managing the health of their patients, but they are also helping to run a business, whether as a solo practitioner or a member of group practice. Therefore, it can be valuable within a PRM platform to offer professionals resources for managing the practice, such as:

    •   training opportunities of all practice members including physicians, nurses, educators, and office staff;

    •   financial management resources for group practices;

- billing assistance, including retrieval of diagnosis and procedure codes, and other relevant forms;

- options for direct product purchase, or direct sample ordering, as appropriate due to regulations;

- ability to directly contact a sales representative, especially relevant for doctors in areas under-served by the sales force.

4. *Community:* this links physicians with peers who have similar practice characteristics and enables sharing of experience. The knowledge shared may be about clinical cases, experience with new medication or products, or other practice-related concerns.

Note that as part of the strategic design of a PRM system, one must consider which of these components should be available to every website visitor, and which of these are only available to registered users. Typically, the product information is likely to be available to all, whereas most of the other features require sign-up.

Registration in a PRM system is typically a more sophisticated *validation* process than is needed for CRM. First, if there are resources that are allowable only for physicians, then the registration form must include space for professional credentials, such as a state license number that authorizes prescribing. Behind the scenes, a database infrastructure must have an updated table to enable this validation. Second, a HCP may be affiliated with multiple group practices that are at distinct addresses. The PRM system design team must determine how many practice addresses may be entered. Aside from this, registration is similar to CRM programs: contact information is collected, there is an opt-in for follow-up communications, and a brief survey may be included for segmentation.

Back to the overall PRM diagram, at the left of the Figure 2.5, we see promotion via multiple channels, placed in locations where the targeted professionals are likely to visit. Since many of the PRM information sources are digital in nature, naturally the primary promotional channels are also electronic. These include banners and search campaigns within HCP websites such as Medscape and E-MPR (Monthly Prescribing Reference), as well as messages within mobile services like Epocrates and QuantiaMD. Each of these can have direct hyperlinks to the PRM website for reviewing services and for registration.

The promotional plan can also quite effectively incorporate traditional channels, also shown in Figure 2.5. Advertisements in professional journals, whether print or electronic, can direct doctors to the PRM website and registration. At medical conventions, a potion of a manufacturing company's booth in the exhibit hall can be allocated to demonstrating the PRM program, and registering interested doctors right on the spot. In addition, the sales representatives who call on each medical professional can also promote the PRM website and services, either via printed materials, or via slides within a tablet PC presentation.

Critical to the promotional plan is a clear message giving reasons for medical professionals to come and register. These reasons are usually the valuable information content available from the website hub which are exclusively available for registered professionals.

For those who register for the PRM system, their information is entered into a PRM database that maintains contact information and logs responses to outbound communications. This PRM database may in turn be connected to the database of the sales force automation system, for coordination of the multiple contacts a healthcare company makes with professionals. This new, integrated communication to physicians requires an underlying technology and data solution that can insure a pharmaceutical company is having a consistent dialogue with each HCP.

The PRM database enables several other processes depicted in Figure 2.5. First, as in a CRM system, a business rules engine controls outbound communication to the professionals by segment. Second, there are campaign analyses that are performed, that track registration rates, and responses to communications. An interesting variation, unique to PRM on the campaign analyses, is the ability to tie physician-level PRM activity to changes in physician-level prescribing of pharmaceutical medications. We will discuss the details of this analysis within the measurement chapters of this book.

A third outcome enabled by the PRM database is a feedback loop that links the non-personal activities of HCPs with the sales representatives that visit them in person. Using the database, a summary of activities on the PRM website can be extracted, and sent in reports to the sales force. This can be achieved at the overall level, or more specifically, by region, city, or for each individual professional. Having this knowledge will help each sales representative be more informed on subsequent calls to their physicians and their practices.

Issues in Developing Relationship Marketing Programs

Now that we have provided an overview of RM programs for both consumers and HCPs, our goal for the remainder of this book is to shed light on the following questions:

- How are RM programs developed?

- How do I prioritize among the many possible in-market tactics that might be required?

- How can I insure coordination among the multiple tactics?

- How can I determine whether my organization is ready to implement such a program?

- What assistance might my company need to insure the RM program runs smoothly?

We will help answer these questions by stepping through a systematic process for developing RM projects. This process, described in the next section, consists of five phases, both for consumer and HCP programs.

The Phases of a Relationship Marketing Project

As illustrated in Figure 2.6, there are five phases in developing a RM program: Discovery, Strategy, Execution, Measurement, and Optimization. Here we overview each phase, paying particular attention to the analytics components.

1. *Discovery*: in the Discovery phase, one performs a competitive assessment, to understand where the product (or company portfolio) being marketed fits within the overall therapeutic category. The business goals of the campaign are discussed; these objectives are typically rooted in the patient or professional

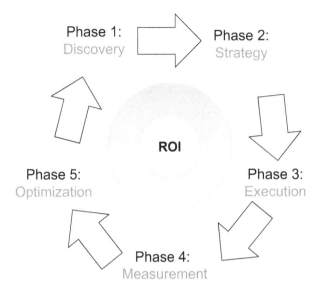

Figure 2.6   Relationship marketing process by phase

journeys, described earlier in this chapter. Additionally, this phase includes understanding the communication channels and media consumption habits of the stakeholders, whether consumers or HCPs. This Discovery phase is also the time to assess the company's readiness for RM from an operations perspective.

2.   *Strategy*: in the Strategy phase of RM, target segments are identified for the program. The major program insight is developed, including the value proposition and offers, which are usually tested in market research. The RM team also develops *personas* of the key segments, and *experience maps* that illustrate the different touch points and messages that these personas will receive, and how they may respond. The media plan is developed here, and in-market tactics are prioritized quantitatively. Also included in the strategic phase is creation of a *measurement plan* that spells out how the RM program will be evaluated versus business goals. The measurement plan may include in-market test of alternative campaign elements.

3.   *Execution*: in the Execution phase, the program is placed into the marketplace. Media is placed, and source coded for tracking effectiveness. The operations playbook is developed, including business rules of which communications are sent under which criteria. Also at the Execution stage, dashboards are designed for tracking campaign performance.

4. *Measurement*: in the Measurement phase, the RM program is assessed along business objectives, as spelled out in the measurement plan. There are multiple quantitative processes here, including promotion response tracking, delivery of performance dashboards, and monitoring of campaign operations. The goals of all of this measurement are twofold. Not only is measurement critical for determining achievement of business goals, but also the measures raise insight for continual improvement (next phase). Ultimately, there is a return on investment (ROI) analysis that evaluates whether the investment in the RM initiative has paid off.

5. *Optimization*: in this fifth stage, the insights from measurement of the campaign are applied toward improvement of the RM program. Operational inefficiencies are addressed, messages and offers can be improved, and target segments can be adjusted. Note that when Optimization has been reached, months or years have passed in the marketplace, and the dynamics of the therapeutic category may have changed. For this reason, in Figure 2.6, Optimization is presented as flowing back into Discovery for the next wave of the RM campaign.

Framing the Rest of This Book

In the chapters that follow, we will go through detailed formalisms and examples for each of these five phases of RM. Within each phase there will be in-depth discussions of programs that serve both consumers and HCPs.

We cannot enumerate every single component of fielding a RM program. For example, creative development, medical legal review, and project schedules will not be covered. However, we will describe in depth the major components where quantitative analysis plays a role.

We will borrow heavily from the principles of direct marketing, foundations of which can be found in Stone and Jacobs (2008) and Wunderman (2004). We will also periodically refer to a host of statistical techniques. For the highly motivated reader who wishes to learn more, it is recommended they consult excellent textbooks in multivariate analysis (Dillon and Goldstein 1984), pattern recognition (Duda, Hart and Stork 2001), data mining (Han and Kamber 2006), and web analytics (Burby and Atchison 2007). For those wishing to learn more about in-depth database development for RM programs, we recommend Todman (2000).

Case Study in Consumer Relationship Marketing

To illustrate the principles of pharmaceutical RM throughout this book, we will develop a case study of CRM and PRM planning for a branded medication. Please note this is intended as a fictitious, yet realistic case study of pharmaceutical marketing. The company, products, and campaigns referred to here are not intended to resemble any actual pharmaceutical marketing scenario.

The case study is about a fictitious company called ABC Pharmaceuticals, and the upcoming June 2011 launch of its new medication for osteoporosis, called "ABCOS." According to the National Osteoporosis Foundation (www. nof.org, 2008 data), the relevant prevalence data is:

- Osteoporosis is a major public health threat for an estimated 44 million Americans, or 55 percent of people aged 50 years or older.

- In the US today, 10 million individuals are estimated to already have the disease and almost 34 million more are estimated to have low bone mass, placing them at increased risk for osteoporosis.

- Of the 10 million Americans estimated to have osteoporosis, eight million (80 percent) are women and two million (20 percent) are men.

Multiple specialties of physicians treat osteoporosis including PCPs, orthopedists, rheumatologists, endocrinologists, and gynecologists. Global sales of osteoporosis treatments, including hundreds of vitamin brands, were nearly $8.4 billion in 2008, according to data from IMS Health.

There are multiple available pharmaceutical therapies in this category, of different mechanisms, forms, and frequencies of dosage. ABCOS is expected to launch to market in six months, and is a non-oral medication that is administered once monthly. ABC Pharmaceuticals is optimistic that the launch will be successful from a conversion and adherence perspective.

The ABCOS brand directors have recognized that this is a crowded market, and will need to establish product awareness among physicians. ABC Pharmaceuticals has planned a sales force of 300 representatives to call on a target list of 45,000 high-prescribing physicians in the osteoporosis category.

ABC Pharmaceuticals is aware that a significant percentage of these physicians may have a "no see policy" and not give time to the representatives.

To address these concerns, in their brand planning presentation, presented in mid-2011 to prepare for 2012 investments, ABC Pharmaceuticals decided to invest in a two-pronged approach to RM in 2012, six months post-launch:

1. A PRM program aimed at specialists and early-adopting PCPs, who can communicate the clinical benefits of ABCOS and share the early experiences of advocates who have begun prescribing by early 2012. The budget for non-personal PRM promotion is $3 million, which is separate from the sales force detailing and starter kit expenses.

2. A CRM campaign, aimed especially at women in the target age range of 45 to 64. The CRM campaign will be multi-channel, will be kicked off with significant media spending in the first half of 2012, and will have a strong call to action. There will be a first-half media plan of $7.5 million, the details of which will be shared in a later chapter.

In the chapters ahead, we will revisit this fictitious case study of ABCOS, and ask homework exercises along the way to reinforce the lessons about CRM and PRM: Discovery, Strategy, Execution, Measurement, and Optimization. Below you may find some introductory questions:

Exercises for Chapter 2

The following questions apply to the expected beginning of the ABCOS RM programs in Q1, 2012:

Question 2.1   Who are the target consumers for ABCOS? What stages of the patient journey are most of these consumers at with respect to ABCOS?

Question 2.2   Who are the target HCPs for ABCOS? What stages of the physician journey are most of these professionals at with respect to ABCOS?

Question 2.3   What are the core components of the CRM system that must be developed for ABCOS?

Question 2.4   What are the core components of the HCP PRM system that must be developed for ABCOS?

3

Discovery: Situation Assessment

In order to develop a healthcare relationship marketing (RM) program, the first phase is called Discovery. In this Discovery phase, one performs a situation assessment to determine:

1. lifecycle analysis for the product or products being marketed;

2. sales or prescription trends within the therapeutic category;

3. trends and forecasts for the particular product or products being marketed;

4. market research available for this category or this product;

5. the competitive landscape of RM activities;

6. media consumption habits of the target audience;

7. conversations among the target audience about the therapeutic class;

8. operational capabilities of the company wishing to deploy the RM campaign.

Analytic techniques and quantitative measurement play a significant role in each of these dimensions of discovery. In this chapter we will proceed in order, and describe the data sources, tools, and analysis techniques employed in this Discovery phase.

Product Lifecycle Considerations

Critical to determining where RM can play a role is an understanding of where in the *product lifecycle* a product is. There are four different stages that are present across most industries, and this framework has been cited in many marketing and product management textbooks, such as Gorchels (2005). These stages are illustrated in Figure 3.1, which graphs the pattern of a typical product's annual sales over time, and are called: *introduction, growth, maturity,* and *decline*. For branded pharmaceuticals in the US, the inflection point between the maturity and decline stages is most often precipitated by a *loss of exclusivity* to market a product, and the concurrent introduction of cheaper generic competitors.

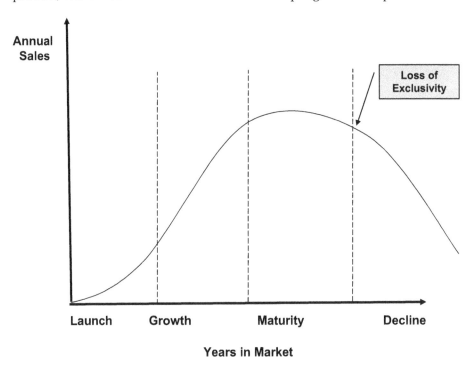

Figure 3.1   The branded pharmaceutical product lifecycle

Depending on the stage of the lifecycle, RM can accomplish particular objectives, whether among consumers or healthcare professionals (HCPs).

- In the introduction (launch) stage, RM can help spread product awareness and insure initial trial with support and feedback to patients and prescribers.

- In the growth stage, RM can accelerate product usage and establish communities between the early adopters and the other high-prescribing "fence sitters" waiting for clinical experience. Natural communities between patients may also form where discussions about medications will take place.

- During the maturity stage and before the loss of exclusivity, RM can play a key role in establishing loyalty to a branded medication before a generic is available, usually by delivering support services and financial programs that encourage repeat usage.

- During the decline phase, there is little role for new RM initiatives. Where possible, existing infrastructure, as inexpensive as possible, can be maintained to harvest branded product sales rather than loss to generic competition.

Sales Forecasts in the Therapeutic Category

In order to estimate the potential impact of a pharmaceutical relationship marketing (RM) program, one needs to first understand the potential sales volume within the therapeutic category, both currently and for several years into the future. The first place to find these sales figures are in pharmaceutical forecasting reports.

Forecasts are helpful for RM assessment because they help marketers understand these issues:

- Is my product among the first within a therapeutic category to come to market in a particular country? If so, then my product's growth potential may be bounded primarily by the number of patients with the disease, and the number of potential prescribing physicians. Also, my RM approach can benefit from unbranded messaging, where communications to patients and doctors emphasize screening for diseases and the benefits of the new medication category. Examples of such situations were:

    - when the first erectile dysfunction oral medications launched in the 1990s; this was a new class of treatment, forecasts were very high, and both CRM programs and physician messaging focused on disease awareness, education, and screening.

- Alternatively, is my product entering a crowded class of drugs, all with similar profiles and mechanism of action? If so, then my sales projections will be primarily bounded based on sales levels achieved by competitors, and achievable market share estimates. The favored RM approach will be branded, with messaging emphasizing the distinct benefits of the new product. Unbranded messaging would be counterproductive, as it would benefit the multiple market leaders. In addition, the new product may want to incorporate value-added services into its RM approach, for both physicians and patients.

  - An example of this scenario is the crowded hyperlipidemia or cholesterol management market of the 2000s and the 2010s, where there are multiple statin drugs, both branded and generic. The advertising messages and RM programs are branded and distinctive.

In this chapter we will cover the basic concepts of pharmaceutical forecasting. A complete derivation of pharmaceutical forecasting is beyond the scope of this book; the reader interested in a more in-depth treatment may read Cook (2006), or may investigate proceedings of the EyeforPharma forecasting workshops over the years.

Global, pipeline forecasts are reports that examine trends in a therapeutic category and project out into the future, generally for the next five years. These forecasts also take into account the pipeline of drugs in research and development that may come to market within the next several years. The projections are typically for the most commercially developed "major markets," which are usually the USA, Canada, Japan, and the largest Western European countries (Germany, France, and the UK, perhaps others). Good sources for global pipeline forecasts include DataMonitor and Decision Resources, as well as financial analysts from individual banks, or compiled financial sources such as Thomson or Reuters. Another pipeline forecasting tool that also incorporates competitive intelligence newswires is called Evaluate Pharma. All of these global pipelines forecasts are based primarily on these factors:

- patient epidemiology by country;

- volume of prescribers within that category;

- historical sales trends of related products;

- the sequence of launching products, by mechanism of action.

Global pipeline forecasting is illustrated in Figure 3.2 and it is a good information source for determining a long-range estimate of expected sales by product and by country. One can also draw information about expected launches of new products by examining the uptake curves for product analogues products that were launched previously. The IMS Health Analogue planner is a database of over 1,000 product launches, organized by country and therapeutic category, and also including attributes like innovation ratings and level of market congestion. The use of analogues is illustrated in Figure 3.3; several products are selected by similarity to a newly launching drug among the dimensions sited above. The uptake curves of each of these products is taken, and all are standardized by percent of peak annual sales. Then a weighted average of the analogues is taken, to estimate how soon a newly launched product may achieve its sales. Multiple forecasting sources can be combined to estimate year-by-year sales of a newly launched product.

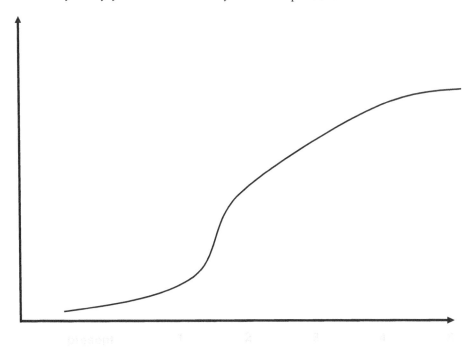

Figure 3.2   Five-year global therapeutic forecast

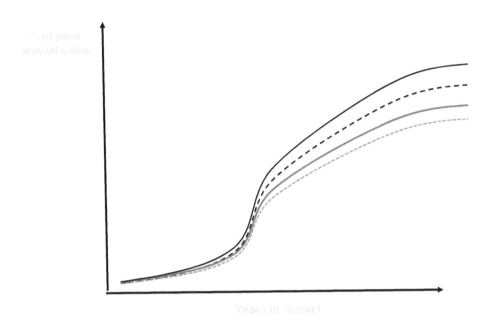

Figure 3.3   Using analogues for peak market share forecasting

Forecasting analyses are not enough to estimate the potential impact of an RM program. In order to do that, one should examine recent prescription trends in the therapeutic category, at various levels of aggregation.

Secondary Prescription and Sales Data

SOURCE OF BUSINESS ANALYSIS

Aside from forecasting sources, one can also directly review historical prescription or sales data in the therapeutic category of interest. The leading data vendors from which to obtain this data are SDI, IMS, or Wolters Kluwer.

One first type of analysis to conduct is a source of business, to determine where prescriptions come from in that category. Sources include:

- Retail pharmacies:

    - these may include regional pharmacy chains, local "mom and pop" pharmacies, or large supermarket wholesalers with pharmacies, such as Target and Wal-Mart.

- Mail order pharmacies:

  - examples of these are Medco, Express Scripts, and Anthem Rx Management. This channel is especially relevant for chronic, daily medications that patients may fill more cheaply in 90-day increments.

- Institutions, including:

  - hospitals;

  - military, such as Veterans Administration hospitals or bases;

  - long-term care centers.

- Specialty pharmacies, for complex medical devices, and certain injections and infusions.

Note that there has been a gradual shift in the sales channels of prescriptions. A study by the Agency for Healthcare Research and Quality (Stagnitti 2008) has shown that of those patients filling a prescription in the US, more than 13 percent received a prescription via mail order pharmacy in 2005, up from 9 percent in 2000. The study notes that, "During the same time frame, the proportion of Americans who bought their prescription medicines from drug stores slipped from 65 percent to 61 percent; from pharmacies in clinics, HMOs, or hospitals declined from 15 percent to 13 percent; and from pharmacies inside supermarkets and super stores like Target and Wal-Mart stores fell from 32 percent to 28 percent." This shift toward mail order is likely due to a rise in chronic, long-term medications among an aging population. Note also that the typical mail order package of a 90-day supply steers toward improved persistence.

There are also variations in source of prescriptions across therapeutic categories. Degenerative conditions affecting the elderly, such as Alzheimer's disease, have significant drug purchases through long-term care centers. Mail order pharmacies are often used for chronic conditions such as hypertension, high cholesterol, or antidepressants, where a 90-day supply for the cost savings is attractive to patients and payers. Knowing the particular channels that medication usage comes from can help in developing tactics for RM.

Prescription data in the US is most often obtained from a sample of retail pharmacies taken from one of the leading data vendors. The sample of prescriptions is roughly 65 percent of all retail prescriptions, and is projected to estimate the total volume of retail prescriptions in the country. Beyond retail, one can also acquire institutional account-level sales data that covers hospitals, long-term care centers, and military bases. This sales data either comes either as extended units of products shipped, or a conversion to US dollars, usually based on wholesale acquisition cost (WAC).

PRESCRIPTION TREND AND MARKET SHARE ANALYSES

Reviewing and understanding prescription trends across products in a therapeutic category can help develop RM programs. One who does so can answer the following critical business questions:

1.   What is the overall prescription volume in the therapeutic category?

    •   This provides an overall market sizing, which can then be multiplied by market share to estimate the potential incremental impact of marketing programs. For example, attaining an incremental 1 percent dollar market share in an $5 billion dollar market means an extra $50 million dollars of sales.

2.   How crowded is the therapeutic category?

    •   If there are many drugs in the category, this will make it more difficult to distinguish with a unique message alone, making it more important to provide RM as a service.

3.   Is there a dominant market leader?

    •   Such a dominant product may have marketing services that are already successful, and can be adapted as you develop your CRM or professional relationship marketing (PRM) strategy.

4.   Is there distinction by subcategories with distinct mechanisms of action?

    •   As an example, consider the different subcategories within the hypertension market (ACE inhibitors, CCBs, and so on) or the rheumatoid arthritis market (NSAIDs, DMARDs, and biologics). One needs to consider how physicians and patients consider each subcategory when treating patients. When designing CRM, one may first establish the benefits of a subcategory, as well as show competitiveness within that subcategory.

- This is also another way to look at market shares, which can be calculated overall, as well as within the smaller subcategory.

5.   How have new product launches fared in this category?

- If you are creating a CRM program for a newly launched product, or one soon to launch, it is beneficial to learn about the adoption curve of other newly launched products. What market share levels did these other products attain in their first year or two, and what consumer and professional promotional campaigns did they try?

6.   Have there been significant market events within the past few years that have abruptly affected prescription trends?

- These may include warnings from the US Food and Drug Administration (FDA), safety concerns, or loss of exclusivity of leading branded products. Any of these will explain sudden market share changes.

- Similarly, it is critical to understand what major events are on the horizon within the next few years: other products coming to market, or other brands losing exclusivity.

- When examining prescription data, two definitions will prove helpful:

  – **NRx** are "new prescriptions," signifying a new order that a patient takes to the pharmacist. Refills are not included. Note, however, even a NRx may be either a new patient start on therapy, or a continuation of existing therapy.

  – **RRx** are "refill prescriptions," which a patient fills without a new order from the doctor.

– **TRx** are "total prescriptions," meaning all medication orders are included, both new and refills.

We thus have the equation **TRx = NRx + RRx**.

We also will refer to the term "market share," defined as:

- A product P's *NRx market share* over a time period T is the sum of product P's NRx over that time period, divided by all product's NRx over that same time period.

- A product P's *TRx market share* over a time period T is the sum of product P's TRx over that time period, divided by all product's TRx over that same time period.

Noteworthy is that newly launched products have virtually no refills within the first few months, making NRx very close to TRx for a new launch, and making the NRx market share greater than TRx market share.

As an example of how to interpret prescription data, consider the prescription data illustrated in Figure 3.4. This is realistic national monthly retail prescription data over a five-year period, in an anonymous therapeutic category. The X-axis timeline is labeled Year 1 (four years ago) through Year 5 (current year). The Y axis represents new prescriptions (NRx) by drug on a monthly basis. From examining this chart, one can surmise several hypotheses about this market:

- It is a crowded therapeutic category filled with seven products across two subcategories based on an original and a newer mechanism of action.

- The overall NRx per month is currently approximately 1.0 million, and has been gradually increasing year over year (a total by month confirms this).

- There were two leading products during years one and two, however, partway into year 2, product B suffered a significant market share drop due to publicized safety concerns.

- There have been three product launches within a new subcategory with a distinctive mechanism of action. The first product launch

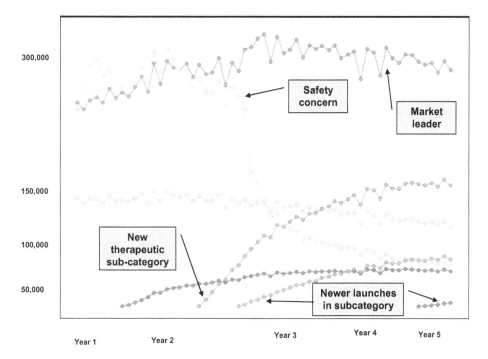

300,000

150,000

100,000

50,000

Safety
concern

Market
leader

New
therapeutic
sub-category

Newer launches
in subcategory

Year 1   Year 2   Year 3   Year 4   Year 5

Figure 3.4   Retail prescription data (NRx) showing market dynamics

during year 2 was very successful. Due to its rapid growth phase,
this new product attained the second highest NRx market share
by year 4. The second and third product launches within the new
subcategory have not had nearly as successful a growth phase to
date.

SPECIALTY VERSUS PRIMARY CARE PRESCRIBING

Breaking out prescription data by physician specialty can be particularly
revealing. For one, specialists as a segment overall have different practice
characteristics to primary care physicians (PCPs):

- there are fewer specialists than PCPs, and their duty may include
  not only prescribing medication, but also surgeries and time
  consuming consultations;

- specialists are often referred the harder-to-treat patients with more
  serious disease progression, and that require the more innovative
  therapies;

- specialists tend to become aware of the newest therapies through specialized medical conventions and medical journals.

As a result, prescribing habits among PCPs and specialists tend to differ, especially when it comes to newly launched products. See Table 3.1 below.

Table 3.1   Comparison of HCP prescribing habits

	Primary Care Physician	Specialist
Quantity	Large: hundreds of thousands	Smaller: thousands or tens of thousands
Prescriptions per MD	Range: small to medium	Range: medium to large
Patient base	General population	Referred, harder-to-treat cases
Adoption of new drugs	Medium to late	Early to medium

For these reasons, in many therapeutic categories, PCPs make up a larger percentage of the overall prescribing, even though specialists write more Rx per physician. Specialists also tend to adopt new products earlier, as they are often referred the harder-to-treat patients that demand innovative therapies.

Upside Potential for Pharmaceutical Relationship Marketing Programs

Now, consider that we are asked to develop CRM and PRM initiatives for Product D, the first product that was launched with a new mechanism of action in some category.

We can use the NRx data in Figure 3.4, with additional parameters, to estimate what our budget should be for RM.

Based on the chart, currently product D still appears in the growth phase, and is averaging roughly 150,000 NRx per month. Let us presume further that for every NRx, prescription data has shown that patients fill 1.5 refills on average. This means each NRx results in 2.5 TRx. Let us further presume that one Rx is used per month, and that the manufacturer makes a net of 80 dollars per monthly Rx.

As a rule of thumb, let us place a range on the annual impact of RM (CRM and/or PRM) at 2 percent to 5 percent of NRx.

We begin our calculations of the sales impact thusly:

- The monthly TRx is for product D is roughly 150,000 × 2.5 = 375,000.

- Annualized for a year this makes estimated annual TRx as: 4,500,000 TRx.

A range of 2 percent to 5 percent impact of RM is 90,600 to 225,000 TRx. Multiplied by $80 yields means that:

- a 2 percent impact on annualized sales is: $7.2 million.

- a 5 percent impact on annualized sales is: $18 million.

Now, consider that the drug manufacturer requires that incremental sales be at least double the investment for any new marketing initiatives. Therefore the range of allowable spending limits for RM is from $3.6 million to $9 million.

Later in this book, in Chapter 7, we shall go into much more depth as to the components of CRM and PRM costs and sales lifts. For now, this brief analysis has shown what parameters and assumptions are critical in determining allowable program budgets.

PATIENT-LEVEL DATA TRENDS

One can also review summarized trends of anonymous patient-level longitudinal data from vendors like SDI, IMS, or Wolters Kluwer. The first trends to examine are related to *source of business*. Some trends to investigate to identify opportunities include:

- *New patient start rates*: when patients receive their first treatments in the therapeutic category, which treatments are they receiving first line? What share of future new patient starts could we hope to attain with the drug we are focusing our CRM program on?

- *Switching from competitors:* some therapeutic categories, like pain relief, are marked by continual switching between medications, as patients seek to find the solution that provides relief. As part of strategy development, think if your drug can develop a message that can support patients switching to the CRM product.

- Anonymous patient-level claims data can also help identify if CRM can make an improvement in adherence.

- *Increased compliance*: what is the trend in this therapeutic category? Are patients taking their medication regularly, as directed, at the proper dosage, and if not, can this be improved via CRM? The most straightforward example of this is a once per day pill, as exists for pain relief, hypertension, or cholesterol management. In this case, review frequency of refills on a 30-day prescription: are these happening every 30 days, or more sporadically? If not, say the refills are happening every 45 days on average. That means 30 pills are being taken in 45 days, for a compliance rate of $30/45 = 2/3 = 67\%$. Now, say a CRM program could increase that compliance rate to 80 percent for 50,000 members at \$3 per pill. That would mean a 90-day compliance impact of:

  - $(80\% \times 90 \text{ pills} - 67\% \times 90 \text{ pills}) \times \$3/\text{pill} \times 50,000 \text{ members}$

  - $= (72 - 60) \text{ pills} \times \$3 \times 50,000 = \$1.8 \text{ Million}$

  Of course, adjustments can be made to these calculations for medications dosed multiple times per day.

- *Increased persistence*: one can determine from anonymous patient-level data what the average persistence, or length of therapy is for the CRM product, or if pre-launch, other products in the category.

- See Figure 3.5 for the layout of a typical persistence curve. The X axis indicated months on therapy, and the Y axis signifies the percentages of patients beginning therapy on a drug that remain on that drug after each month. For the hypothetical medication Z in the figure, we see that 90 percent of those starting therapy on Z obtain their first refill, and only 68 percent of those beginning therapy on Z obtain their second refill. For some reason, the second refill on Z has proven a significant drop-off point. This may be due in part to a variety of reasons, including:

  - lack of perceived efficacy in the short term;

  - unclear expectations on the patient regarding side effects;

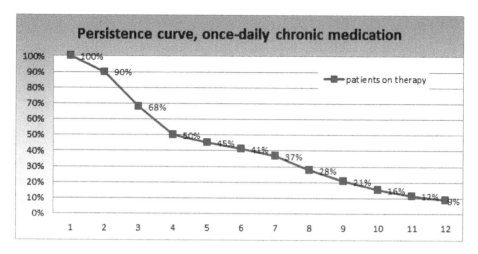

Figure 3.5   Patient persistence curve

–   cost issues;

–   switching of patients to another therapy.

The percentages of patients remaining on therapy Z, in fact, decreases further, down to 50 percent at month 3, and then steadily lower percentages thereafter. Clearly, there is a significant opportunity if persistence can be increased in months two or three. In order to quantify this opportunity, we need to introduce the right terminology and calculations.

From this persistence curve and the monthly compliance data, we can define two valuable measures. Let P(t) be the percentage of patients persistent to at least month t. Then first, let the *average length of therapy* on a medication:

$$Average\ length\ of\ therapy = \sum_{t=1}^{Tmax} t * [P(t) - P(t+1)]$$

The average length of therapy is weighted sum of the month count *t* times the percentage of patients on therapy for exactly that month count. This sum continues up until the maximum number of months that patients can remain on therapy. Note that P(Tmax + 1) is zero, so that the last addend in the equation is Tmax * P(Tmax). This represents the remaining percentage of people that have persisted over the entire course of therapy.

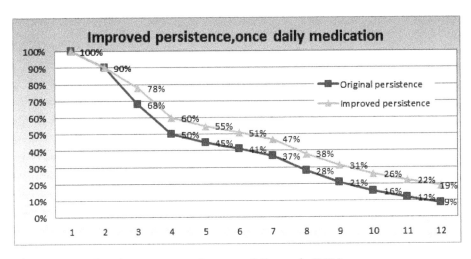

Figure 3.6   **Persistence curve improved through CRM**

For Figure 3.6 (above), showing length of therapy on medication Z, the average length of therapy is 5.2 months, if we presume 12 months is the maximum duration on therapy. Now, if we can improve the percentage on therapy Z of patients during month three and beyond ten percentage points across the board, that will increase up to 5.2 months. This difference is illustrated in Figure 3.6.

The other calculation that helps us quantify opportunity is *average lifetime value of a patient on therapy.* Say the monthly persistence percentage at month t is P(t) and the monthly compliance (measured by doses taken) at month t is C(t), and let the value per dose (for example, per pill) be a fixed constant V. Then, the average lifetime value of a patient on a particular drug appears below

$$Lifetime\ value = \sum_{t=1}^{Tmax} P(t) * C(t) * V$$

In other words, the Lifetime value is the summed value of compliant doses by month across all those patients who are still persistent to that month.

Let us return to the example in Figure 3.6, and add the additional parameters:

-     revenue of \$3.00 per pill;

- monthly compliance ranges from 24 pills per month for those patients lasting just a few months on therapy, up to 27 pills per month for those patients that last 10 months or more on therapy.

Then, based on a maximum length of therapy of 12 months, the lifetime value can be calculated as shown in Table 3.2.

Table 3.2   Sample lifetime value calculation

Months	Patients on therapy	Monthly compliance	Revenue
1	100%	24	$72.00
2	90%	24	$64.80
3	68%	24	$48.96
4	50%	25	$37.50
5	45%	25	$33.75
6	41%	25	$30.75
7	37%	26	$28.78
8	28%	26	$21.59
9	21%	26	$16.19
10	16%	27	$12.61
11	12%	27	$9.46
12	9%	27	$7.09
		Lifetime value	$383.48

Therefore, the lifetime value of new patients starting on this medications is $383.48. This can be a multiplying factor within an incremental sales calculation for a CRM program, even without any increase in persistence or compliance. For example, if a CRM program can convert 20,000 new patients on to this medication, the impact of that alone is: 20,000 * $383.48 = $7.67 million.

In reality, many medications do not have a hard and fast Tmax, the longest applicable month on therapy, and if this does exist, it may be much more than a year. We have used Tmax = 12 for conceptual simplification. For a therapy intended to be taken for 5 years, then one would use Tmax = 60. Practically speaking, however, in the month of therapy where the percentage of persistent patients gets close to zero, that month is a Tmax.

Understanding compliance and persistence issues identifies two significant areas of impact that CRM can achieve. Understanding how to compute lifetime value of a new patient on therapy enables calculation of incremental sales, which is a critical component of return on investment (ROI).

Primary Market Research Results

As part of the discovery process leading to RM planning, it is important to directly hear the attitudes, preferences, and points of view of the actual stakeholders, especially patients and HCPs. Hearing firsthand the concerns of these stakeholders about healthcare experiences and marketed therapies can enable solutions on how RM can enhance those experiences and position a medication for success.

CONSUMER MARKET RESEARCH

From the standpoint of developing RM programs, primary market research can help in understanding what patients and caregivers really experience as they navigate through the patient journey. We discussed this patient journey back in Chapter 2, and mentioned that a major objective of RM is to try to move patients along the stages from left to right.

This book will not attempt to provide an in-depth treatment of pharmaceutical market research. Those readers requiring a more detailed study of primary research methodology should consult a recent textbook such as Creswell (2009).

Qualitative research consists of structured interviews to ask consumers about some or all stages of the patient journey within a particular therapeutic area. Each respondent is asked to describe their current clinical situation, and to expound on their particular experiences to date. The goal is to uncover particular issues that may be standing in the way of conversion to treatment, or adherence on that treatment. Additionally, qualitative primary research can uncover particular language on how consumers express their issues, challenges, and hurdles. In-depth interviews (IDIs) are conducted one on one with individual consumers, whereas focus groups are moderated discussions with a set of consumers at a similar stage of the patient lifecycle. Thus, in discovery research that prepares for a CRM program for diabetes treatment Z, there may be one focus group with one focus group made up of patients who have been treated with a competitor's medication who may have the opportunity to switch to treatment Z, and another focus group of patients who have recently started to take treatment Z, to assess issues related to adherence.

Note that consumers may either be patients or caregivers. Within therapeutic categories that require caregivers, such as oncology or degenerative mental diseases, it can be quite valuable to obtain the perspective of caregivers as well. Caregivers may be the individuals reading the CRM materials and encouraging the patients to take a certain course of action, or even making decisions on behalf of the patients.

Quantitative research typically comes after qualitative, and consists of survey instruments sent to a larger cohort of patients or caregivers. A screening questionnaire insures that participants are similar enough, such as patients with Type 2 diabetes who have tried at least one prescription medication. The volume of patients in the survey is computed via a "power calculation" to find a minimum sample size to reach a certain statistical significance. Surveys may be conducted in person, over the telephone, or over the Internet.

The questions within the survey are typically multiple-choice, potentially supplemented with several open-ended questions allowing free text comments. The intent of the questions is to assign quantitative percentages of patients or caregivers that may have a particular attitude, or that might make a particular decision, that has come up in qualitative research. For example, a question might be:

> *"If a once-weekly subcutaneous injection were available to help control your blood glucose levels, and would replace the need for a daily pill, how likely would you be to ask your doctor about this treatment?"*

> *Not at all likely*
> *Somewhat likely*
> *Likely*
> *Very likely*
> *Extremely likely.*

Details of how to design and analyze market research surveys may be found in Alreck and Settler (2003).

The analysis of quantitative research results can help developing CRM in several ways. First, the survey results can help in pro-forma analyses. Knowing that 78 percent of patients surveyed answered very likely or extremely likely (also called "top two box") to the above question provides a multiplicative factor in the treatment chain estimator: once aware of the new once-weekly treatment, 78 percent will ask their doctor about it. Secondly, the survey results can help in segmentation planning, especially when combined with other demographic or behavioral background questions. For example, by combining the above question with another that asks: "How long have you been diagnosed with type 2 diabetes?" may start to get at differentiated communications strategies by segment. Additionally, survey results may help in choosing among CRM campaign messages or services. A question like: "Which of the following services may help you in managing your diabetes?" followed by multiple choices, can help in ranking and prioritizing CRM program elements.

PROFESSIONAL MARKET RESEARCH

Professional market research consists of essentially the same techniques as consumer market research, described in the section above, except of course they are conducted with HCPs. An important distinction is that for PRM, we are trying to learn more about the HCP journey, described in Chapter 2. Thus, the research tries to understand the attitudes and motivations that professionals have around a particular condition, in particular:

- how they acquire the latest information on new therapies;

- how they communicate with patients who have a particular condition;

- their perspectives on trial, and adoption of medications and other therapies.

As with consumers, qualitative focus groups or IDIs usually proceed with quantitative survey research. As with consumers, the surveys may be conducted in person, by telephone, or online, and a host of market research providers are available that cover each channel.

The quantitative research may stand alone for marketing to physicians, or it may dovetail patient research. Consider the following question:

"If your patients who take a daily pill for controlling their blood glucose levels asked you to consider switching them by prescribing a once-weekly subcutaneous injection instead, how likely would you be to prescribe this weekly treatment?"

Not at all likely
Somewhat likely
Likely
Very likely
Extremely likely.

The results from such a question would provide marketers with another estimator in a CRM or PRM pro-forma model. Say, for example, that the responses to the "top two box" above was 60 percent. Then, if relationship marketing and other promotion is used, if physicians are made aware of the new treatment, and if suitable patients are encouraged to ask their physicians for that treatment, the estimate of the number of patients that might be treated with the new therapy would be 60 percent.

Researching Media Consumption Habits

In developing RM programs, a critical design decision is what channels are employed to communicate with your targets. This decision has significant financial consequences from two perspectives:

- the cost of placing media, which can range from hundred of thousands of dollars to tens of millions;

- the incremental sales from responders that convert to therapy, which as shown above, can range from millions to tens of millions of dollars.

As a result, selecting the right media is critical. During Discovery, this should start with understanding the media consumption habits of your target audience.

For consumers, there is unquestionably a trend toward increasing medical information consumption online. A December 2007 study by iCrossing and Opinion Research Corp (Elkin 2008) demonstrated the definitive and growing role that the Internet has in American's search for healthcare information, and the specific role that each online channel plays. Quite noteworthy is that 59 percent of Americans had used Internet resources within the past 12 months to access health and wellness-related information, slightly ahead of the 55 percent of those who went to doctors. However, in terms of trust factor for definitive decision making, HCPs are paramount: 77 percent of consumers stated PCPs were among the top three most trusted sources of information; next were specialty physicians (55 percent), nurse practitioners (37 percent), and pharmacists (36 percent). Only 24 percent felt that Internet resources were among the top three most trusted sources of information. In a similar question, 49 percent of consumers described Internet resources as very important or extremely important in influencing medication decisions, well behind doctors (91 percent), pharmacists (79 percent) or nurse practitioners (78 percent). From a media standpoint, this means that consumers are reachable online as seekers of health information; it also means that the medical messages placed online should aim for patient trust and should work synergistically with the need to seek attention from HCPs.

To get to specific consumer media locations for CRM, there are multiple panel-based research databases that can provide the likelihood of consumers with particular demographics viewing various media sources and events. A traditional source in recent decades has been the Simmons panel (now from Experian), which links consumption of media properties with usage of a wide array of products and services across industries. MARS is a consumer syndicated healthcare study in the US from KMR (Kantar Health) that provides therapeutic category-specific demographics and multi-channel media consumption, including print, television, and Internet. ComScore Media Metrix is an online panel that tracks consumers' website visits across a wide array of industries and summarizes demographic, behavioral, and product interest.

For those wishing to explore HCP media habits, there are similar panel-based studies from Kantar Health that provide relative percentages of sources where physicians, by specialty, obtain their medical information, such as journals, conferences, websites, e-details, healthcare-dedicated TV, direct mail, and newsletters. There are breakouts by digital versus offline versions of media, and trends over the years. These comparative percentages can prioritize channel selection for professional direct response communications.

Note that over the years there has been a dynamic marketplace of data suppliers of consumer and professional media consumption data. However, the objective is always to determine the most likely media channel by which to reach consumers and professionals within your demographic.

While these sources are directional, they do not substitute for a full media plan which is usually prepared by a specialized media agency, with reach and frequency numbers. We will discuss media plans within in Chapter 4 (Strategy).

Search Engine Patterns

In the same study of consumer patterns when seeking healthcare information (Elkin 2008), online search engines were selected as the online resource most frequently used to locate health and wellness-related information (67 percent), ahead of healthcare portals (45 percent), and social media (33 percent).

Furthermore, in terms of frequency, 63 percent of consumers seek health and wellness-related information online at least once a month. As a result, during CRM discovery, search engine analysis is usually an insightful exercise, to understand how consumers are seeking answers related to specific medical conditions.

- When consumers use search engines to find information on medically related topics, they are usually expressing some kind of intent, somehow related to the patient journey. There are several reasons why a consumer may have performed these searches:

    - patients may have recently been diagnosed with a particular condition, and want to learn more about the prognosis, and potential treatments;

    - patients may have just been given a medication to treat a disease, and want to find out more about what to expect while taking that medication.

These categories are substantiated by the "How America searches" study (Elkin 2008), where the top five types of health and wellness-related topics searched for online were: symptoms (60 percent), treatments (58 percent), diseases/conditions (56 percent), wellness (46 percent), and drugs/medications (42 percent).

The relative frequency of terms searched for at each stage of the patient journey can help guide the marketer in how to reach to online consumer. To tease these distinctions out, one can conduct a search engine volume and topic analysis, employing the keyword tool from Google Adwords. This free software enables online marketers to determine estimated frequencies of search terms related to *seed terms* that are provided.

For example, consider fibromyalgia, a condition which causes millions of patients to suffer with chronic, widespread pain for years, before being properly diagnosed by a specialist. Suppose one were designing an unbranded consumer RM campaign that was aimed at educating long-time pain sufferers that their symptoms may be a sign of fibromyalgia, and that they should speak to their physicians. Questions that arise before developing this campaign are:

- How many consumers are seeking information regarding widespread, chronic pain?

- What specific phrases are consumers using as they search for information?

Note that as we are considering an unbranded campaign for those in the pre-diagnosis stage of the patient journey, that we do not expect explicit use of "fibromyalgia" or any of the specific medications that are used to treat it.

A search analysis conducted during 2009, using the Google keyword tool, tried to uncover the volume of searches and the range of language that may shed light on this pre-diagnosis stage. A handful of seed terms included "chronic pain" and "widespread pain" among others. Details of the results are shown in Figure 3.7.

The results of the search were a total of 211 keyword phrases representing 95.7 million search terms per year. However, upon systematic examination of the results, most of these were not associated with the specific symptoms of fibromyalgia. Pain is associated with many conditions, and these search results gave a full range of pain types that consumers may search for. Therefore, the

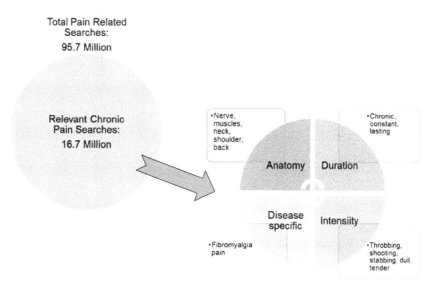

Total Pain Related
Searches:
95.7 Million

Relevant Chronic
Pain Searches:
16.7 Million

•Nerve,
muscles,
neck,
shoulder,
back

Anatomy   Duration

•Chronic,
constant,
lasting

Disease
specific   Intensiity

•Fibromyalgia
pain

•Throbbing,
shooting,
stabbing, dull,
tender

Figure 3.7   Search patterns for pre-diagnosis fibromyalgia
Source: Google Keyword Tool.

next step was a manual filtering exercise, where each search phrase was read to isolate those terms that could be consistent with the symptoms of fibromyalgia. Terms removed from consideration included those clearly representing other types of pain such as "side pain," "arm pain," "back ache," and "jaw pain," as well as other non-descript pain terms such as "left pain," "right pain," and "sharp pain."

After filtering, the number of relevant search terms that are consistent with some of the symptoms of fibromyalgia was 16.7 million, or 17 percent of the original total. This total is remarkable in that the US prevalence of fibromyalgia is estimated at 3 million to 6 million, according to the American College of Rheumatology and the National Institute of Arthritis And Musculoskeletal And Skin Diseases (NIAMS). Therefore, the number of plausible searches is roughly four times the US prevalence.

Certainly, not all of these searches can be proven to come from patients with undiagnosed fibromyalgia. Even with another factor of four reduction, we have a volume of searches on Google that exceeds the target population.

As a result, it can be hypothesized that fibromyalgia is a condition where patients are actively searching for answers and want to find out the root causes of their pain and how to treat it. What also becomes relevant is the multi-faceted language that suffering patients use to describe their pain, along these dimensions:

- time: "chronic pain," "constant pain";

- intensity: "throbbing pain," "shooting pain," "stabbing pain";

- anatomy: "nerve pain," "neck and shoulder pain," "muscle pain";

- seeking causes: "fibromyalgia pain."

These language cues can help in developing a creative strategy for a fibromyalgia campaign, because using phrases like these will resonate with patients looking for answers

As for search term analysis for HCPs, the challenge is lack of available data. At the time of writing this book, search analysis data is not widespread for HCP media sources. Certainly, the leading electronic medical journals and professional social networking sites have search engines, but data on the frequency of search phrases are not readily available. However, the availability of this data may evolve over time.

Social Media Analysis for Healthcare

During the Discovery phase of relationship marketing, the analysis of social media conversations is valuable in helping to answer the following questions:

- What are the categories of discussions taking place related to a particular therapeutic category?

- Where online are consumers discussing these issues? Are they general discussion boards, micromedia like Twitter, demographic specific-interest groups (like motherhood websites), or more specific medical web portals?

- Are there influential patient opinion leaders who publish widely about their experiences with a particular disease, and have a large following?

- How rapidly does news spread over social media? If there is a recent research development, publicity, or news about a medication, how quickly do consumers pass this information along? This is particularly pervasive on "micromedia" social sites like Facebook and Twitter, where users can almost immediately copy, paste and re-post the messages they read to their hundreds of "friends" or "followers."

In a review by Forrester research from early 2009 (Vittal 2009), a wide array of commercial software tools are described are specifically aimed at analyzing patterns of conversations in social media. These software tools are sometimes called *listening platforms*. Some examples of these are Radian6, Buzz Metrics, Visible Technologies, and Listenlogic. Typical listening platform software provides these services:

- retrieving a huge sample of posts from various social media sources, based on query terms or phrases;

    Note that some "spam filtering" is required in the pharmaceutical space to reduce inappropriate posts. For example, you want to screen out free offers for drugs, so remove terms like "free" and "cheap" if you do not need them. Also recommended is filtering out various branded anti-depressants and erectile dysfunction medications, if those are not required. These tend to show up gratuitously in spam postings.

- returning frequencies of posts by phrases representing topic areas;

- providing sentiment on a percentage of the posts, denoting a positive or negative affect toward that topic;

- exporting a set of social media postings that meet a particular query on search terms or format.

As noted in Haimowitz and Obata (2009), there is a disciplined approach to analyzing social media within the pharmaceutical space:

1. First, one must define the business questions that are being explored. These are usually expressed in terms of the patient journey within a particular therapeutic category.

2.   Second, one should establish a taxonomy of the phrases that are expected. Usually this social media taxonomy includes categories like: emotions, symptoms, disease category comments, pharmaceutical treatments, natural therapies, and cost concerns.

3.   Third, when the social media posts are retrieved, noteworthy phrases, or terms, should be extracted, scored by frequency and broken down into the aforementioned categories.

4.   Fourth, arrange results visually. Phrases can be linked with line segments, or arranged in space so that it can be seen which phrases are often mentioned together.

To answer questions like "where" and "by whom" are the conversations happening, one can extract from the downloaded data sets the most frequent website domains, as well as the leading individual posters.

As an example, let's consider the example of fibromyalgia used in our search engine keyword analysis of the previous section. Say our business strategy is aligned with unbranded acquisition and we wish to understand the conversations of those patients who have suffered for years with chronic pain and finally were diagnosed with fibromyalgia.

A social media crawl will reveal:

1.   A wide range of pertinent phrases, including:

   •   descriptions of the pain, as were found in the search analysis: duration, intensity, anatomy;

   •   emotions like frustration, concern, and despair often being mentioned concurrently with the symptoms;

   •   a wide range of misdiagnosed disorders like Lyme disease, Lupus, fatigue, and depression;

   •   the term "Fibromyalgia" itself together with "diagnosis" and associated positive emotional terms as to when the diagnosis is made, like "relief;"

- associated with Fibromyalgia, terms related to "treatment," or "management" as well as actual medications.

2. Frequent bloggers across a wide range of domains who are describing their personal journeys with fibromyalgia, including the road to diagnosis, and how they are currently treating and coping.

3. Fibromyalgia associations and patient support groups, with websites and other social media presences like Facebook pages.

The overall impression from such a social media review reveals that Fibromyalgia is the basis of a very active online patient community, where patients share their experiences both before and after diagnosis, and during ongoing treatment. Specific language can be discovered that would help in developing a creative campaign that speaks directly to patients with an empathetic tone in their own language. Furthermore, the fibromyalgia associations, advocacy groups, and frequent bloggers may be strategic partners to consider as one plans a RM program.

Figure 3.8 is a schematic of what a visual map of the social media terms may look like. Actual results will vary based on the time period analyzed.

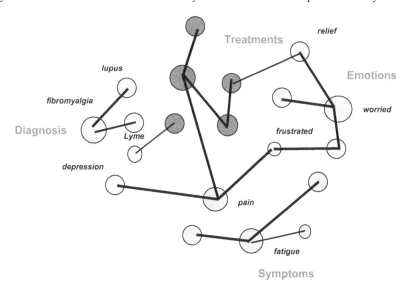

Figure 3.8   Fibromyalgia social media results, illustrated

Other consumer social media searches may have significantly different results. For example, on any pediatric-related disorder, there will be an overwhelming volume of discussions from motherhood and expectant mother social media sites. This applies to allergies, infant formula, antibiotics, and vaccines.

For professional RM discovery, there are an increasing number of social media websites with communities or discussion boards, including Sermo, Medscape, and Ozmosis. Leading topics covered include treatments for patient vignettes, discussion of medications, practice business, and managed care. At the time of writing this book, there is not a professional social media query tool, mainly because these social media sites require the user to log in. However, manual review by appropriately trained and credentialed personnel can be revealing for discovery, to get the perspective and language used by physicians, nurses, and other clinicians.

Operational Needs Assessment for Healthcare Relationship Marketing

For companies developing a new capability in CRM, it is critical in the Discovery phase to perform an internal operational needs assessment. This is a review of company capabilities in CRM from the perspective of infrastructure, processes, and organizational commitment. The outcome of this assessment is a scorecard versus industry benchmarks, and a gap analysis of what other infrastructure, resources, and processes are required for CRM. Needs assessments are generally performed in conjunction with a third-party unbiased consultant that can offer advice based on experience.

The components of the needs assessment usually consists of structured interviews and inventories of company assets. As a minimum, four critical capabilities should be reviewed, as illustrated in Figure 3.9: operational systems, information assets, campaign management, and analytical processes. For each of these, we will itemize particular questions that should be answered during the assessment.

1.   Operational systems

- Is there a CRM database in place that is Health Insurance Portability and Accountability Act (HIPAA) compliant?

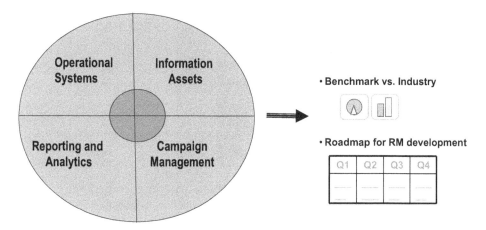

Figure 3.9   Operational needs assessment during relationship marketing discovery

- Are there automated feeds into the established database from all promotional sources that capture contact information: websites, business reply cards, and call centers?

- For PRM, is there a database that houses all of the marketing transactions that reach professionals: e-details, website portal visits, convention contacts?

- If PRM data exists, how integrated is this PRM database with the more traditional data that includes physician-level prescribing and sales force calls, samples, and details?

2.   Information assets

- Is there a periodic data cleansing process that insures consumer contact information remains valid, leveraging national change of address (NCOA), email change of address (ECOA), and related software?

- Is there a systematic process for merging duplicate customers, also known as record matching, or "merge purge" software?

- Does your company invest in third-party data appends for matching to consumer or professional records? This includes demographic and psychographic data that may provide more insights into segmentation.

3. Campaign management capabilities

    •   Does your company have a discipline of developing explicit flow charts of how information is gathered, stored, and managed among systems?

    •   Are campaigns implemented with source coding, so that responses may be measured by promotional tactic?

    •   Does your firm leverage business rules software, which can specify which customer segments are selected to receive which communications over time?

    •   Is there a weekly process of monitoring campaigns for quality assurance?

4. Analytical processes

    •   Does your RM database have a query and reporting system to extract information on a weekly or monthly basis?

    •   Are reporting templates and dashboards used for efficiency and rapid identification of insights?

    •   Are in-depth analyses done that tie together CRM and PRM responses by channel, and promotional behaviors by patients and professionals over time?

    •   Are analytic results shared throughout the company, to identify true insights, and to plan campaign improvements like media optimization and website adjustments?

The output of the operational assessment is a report that summarizes company readiness for developing RM programs, for consumers and/or professionals. Experienced consultants will also be able to deliver:

    •   a benchmark against other companies in the industry;

- a roadmap for how a company can achieve its RM goals, with options for investment.

If significant investment and corporate change are required, then this cannot come all at once. Therefore the quarter-by-quarter roadmap is critical, to prioritize a phased approach and staged investments. We will say more about this in the chapter on Execution (Chapter 6).

Exercises for Chapter 3

DISCOVERY FOR OUR CASE STUDY OF ABCOS

The following exercises are related to a realistic Discovery phase related to the re-launch of our hypothetical osteoporosis medication called ABCOS, from ABC Pharmaceuticals, which was first introduced at the end of Chapter 2. As you will recall, ABCOS is a non-oral medication that has an extended duration of efficacy, and needs to be administered with less frequency than daily. The launch is planned for June 2011 and both PRM and CRM to begin in January 2012. Using the principles we have discussed in this chapter, we invite the reader to develop answers for the following questions. Your solutions may be general, or you may take initiative and actually investigate the osteoporosis category. Answers are in Appendix A.

Question 3.1 What relevant prescription data should be gathered to help understand the market dynamics relevant to ABCOS? What are the relevant specialties?

Question 3.2 What market research should ABC Pharmaceuticals be conducting related to the osteoporosis category. Consider both consumer research and HCP research.

Question 3.3 How can we better understand the online behaviors of consumers in the osteoporosis market in general, and what might that teach us to plan for the ABCOS CRM launch?

Question 3.4 What forecasting may be relevant to the upcoming launch of ABCOS?

Question 3.5 ABC Pharmaceuticals wants to understand if it has the operational capabilities for CRM and PRM. ABC has sales force databases and reporting systems, and has sent email and direct mail to physicians in the past. They have also once piloted a consumer co-pay discount offer for another product. What are the different operational and infrastructure considerations that ABC Pharmaceuticals must face for CRM and PRM related to the ABCOS campaigns?

4

Strategy: Planning the Relationship Marketing Program

In this chapter we will overview the process of developing the strategy for a healthcare relationship marketing (RM) program. The strategy consists of:

- business and brand objectives;

- segmentation;

- experience planning by segment;

- behavior modification objectives;

- strategic insights;

- campaign creative and messaging.

These topics are inter-related, and in an actual RM assignment the strategy is developed for each simultaneously. Furthermore, these aspects of strategic development apply equally to programs for consumers as well for professionals. In this chapter we will interleave discussions of these two stakeholders.

Additionally, to gain a sense of grounding and experience, we also include within this chapter two in-depth interviews with industry experts in different aspects of RM strategy development.

Business and Brand Objectives

For RM, business objectives are usually expressed in terms of the patient journey and the professional journeys that we have discussed in Chapter 2. These stages in turn are based on where the brand is within the product lifecycle, which we introduced in Chapter 3. Table 4.1 summarizes the objectives by stage of the product lifecycle.

Table 4.1   Relationship marketing objectives by stage of product lifecycle

Product Lifecycle	Consumer Relationship Marketing Objectives	Professional Relationship Marketing Objectives
Pre-Launch	Perhaps unbranded	Share clinical data
Launch	Awareness and conversion	Awareness and trial Complement sales force
Growth	Wider conversion Adherence	Broader trial Adoption Advocacy by early adopters
Maturity	Continued conversion Adherence Advocacy	Regular prescribing Broader adoption Broader advocacy Relationship and service
Decline/LOE	Deeper relationships Loyalty to brand	Deeper relationships Loyalty to brand, to company, to category portfolio

- During *pre-launch*, consumer relationship marketing (CRM) is either unbranded or not yet implemented. However, it can be quite critical to communicate with the healthcare professional (HCP) community on clinical data, through non-personal promotion (NPP), journals, and conventions, to prepare the market for launch.

- During *introduction or product launch*, the goal for both consumers and professionals is to achieve product awareness and trial. Patients should be made aware of the new therapy and encouraged to discuss the treatment with their doctor. HCPs must be made aware of the treatment, by the sales force as well as NPP, so that this can be prescribed when the appropriate patient is seen.

- During the *growth phase*, the goal is broader conversion to therapy among patients, and adherence to therapy among those already on therapy. There may also be advocacy among early patients, through social media, in a spontaneous setting. For HCPs, the goal is more widespread adoption, and for early adopting physicians to become local advocates amongst other professionals.

- During the *maturity phase*, the goal is expanded conversion and adherence among the patient base, and there is opportunity for a structured, moderated advocacy program among patients. The goal for HCPs is not only for broader product prescribing among a wider set of physicians, but also to build a deeper relationship with professionals beyond that of a product manufacturer, to a consultant providing services for the professional practice.

- During the *decline phase* (including loss of exclusivity), the goal for both consumers and HCPs is brand loyalty, and leveraging the relationships built for future product launches. In the case of HCPs, a pharmaceutical company may wish to insure a good company relationship with the practice for the future. One example of this is to establish a portfolio credential in the therapeutic category, especially if future products in that category are imminent.

Special Consideration: Product or Portfolio Relationship Marketing?

As part of strategic development, one must determine the scope of the RM program. Two alternatives are:

- *Single product*: when a pharmaceutical manufacturer has just one marketed product within a therapeutic category, and no other products on the near-term horizon, then most likely the RM program will be branded for that product alone.

- *Portfolio*: when there are multiple products (either in-market or nearing launch) within a single therapeutic category, a pharmaceutical manufacturer may also consider a portfolio RM program. The benefit of a portfolio RM program is being able to maintain relationships with patients or HCPs as multiple products come to market. There is also more upside potential to address unbranded disease awareness and educational topics when a company has multiple products in that category.

- Even for multiple related conditions, a portfolio approach may be of interest. Consider the overlapping cardiovascular-related conditions like hypertension, hyperlipidemia, diabetes, and erectile dysfunction. High volumes of patients have more than one of these conditions. A common CRM platform speaking to all of these conditions can provide valuable services to a core set of patients over time, and contribute to multiple medication usage.

For the rest of this book, we will make the presumption that we are developing a RM program for a single product. However, where there are extensions or enhancements for a portfolio of products, we shall raise these where appropriate.

Segmentation Strategy Development

Earlier in this chapter we outlined the patient journey for a particular therapeutic category. However, not all consumers with a medical condition will have the same background, nor will they interact with the same HCPs or have the same set of experiences. Consequently a CRM program should not be designed as one-size-fits-all. Rather, CRM programs are nearly always designed for multiple segments.

The dimensions of segmentation relevant to CRM are illustrated in Figure 4.1, and include:

- Demographics, including age, gender, geography, income, and occupation. Also important to note is whether the consumer is a patient, or a caregiver for another patient that is making treatment decisions.

- Clinical history, including what HCPs the patient has seen, what symptoms they have.

- Attitudes and motivations that influence the patient to take action. These have been described separately in Chapter 1.

To illustrate with an example, say a pharmaceutical brand marketing team is trying to launch a new drug for Type II diabetes. One can think of multiple

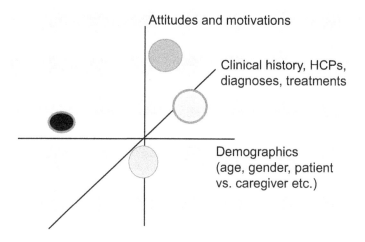

Figure 4.1   **Segmentation for consumer relationship marketing programs**

segments of consumers that might participate in a Type II diabetes program. Two examples are:

1.   Women in their 60s who have been diagnosed over a decade ago, are seeing a cardiologist and endocrinologist, and regularly treat with insulin.

2.   Young men in their 30s who are first diagnosed with diabetes by their primary care physician.

These segments are quite distinct in terms of their influences, clinical history, and media habits. Plus, there are other segments. How does a brand marketing team know which of the segments they should be marketing to? Analytics and quantification are critical to determining which segment should be the focus, or *target,* of a RM campaign.

QUANTITATIVE MARKET RESEARCH FOR SEGMENTATION

Consumer segments may be thought of and discussed conceptually, but in fact segments are distinct sets of data points. As such, segments should be developed from a quantitative research and analysis. Typically, quantitative primary market research should be carried out with a large sample size, at least several hundred participants. In this book, we provide a basic overview of quantitative primary market research for segmentation. For a more detailed description, please see a textbook such as Creswell (2009) or Alreck and Settle (2003).

The process for such segmentation research is illustrated in Figure 4.2. First, the correct eligible consumer population must be determined. For example, consider a pharmaceutical brand with an indication for migraine treatment in adults that wants to develop a relevant consumer segmentation. Research would begin, via the telephone or the Internet, applying screening criteria to determine consumers who have experienced migranes. Those consumers who pass the screening process would then be asked a series of questions related to their demographics, attitudes and methods of treating migraine. Possible questions could include:

- What is your age? Your gender?

- How intense is your typical migraine on a scale of 1 to 10?

- Which specialties of HCP have you consulted with?

- Which drugs have you taken?

The number of questions per research respondent may be several dozen or more. Typically, the questions are multiple-choice, but may also be rankings or cardinal answers (such as low, medium, or high). Once the questionnaires are completed, the result will form a quantitative data set for further analysis. The data set has one record per consumer and one column for the response to each question, as illustrated in Figure 4.2.

In order to develop segments from this data set, a series of steps must be applied. First, the data should be cleansed, to filter out suspect responders, such as those leaving many questions blank or those whose answers are inconsistent across questions. Another part of cleansing may include standardization or

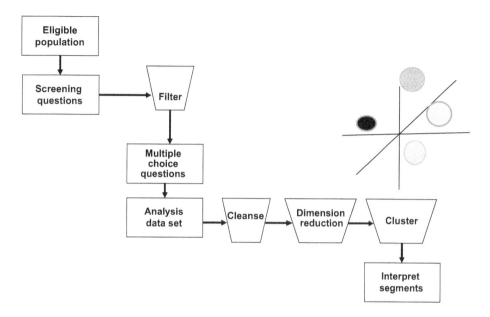

Figure 4.2   Schematic of quantitative primary market research

normalization of variables, and creation of "dummy variables" for responses to multiple-choice questions. Second, the researcher should apply *dimensionality reduction* to bring down the number of dimensions in the data, and make the variables less correlated with each other. Vectors that are completely uncorrelated are said to be independent or orthogonal. Several techniques for reducing dimensions in multivariate data may be found in Duda, Hart and Stork (2001) or Dillon and Goldstein (1984). These include:

- principal components analysis, which creates new dimensions that are orthogonal;

- factor analysis, which also creates new dimensions, though not usually orthogonal;

- viewing correlation matrices among the column vectors, and selecting one item among highly correlated variables. This method maintains variable names and meanings.

Following dimensionality reduction, the data set has far fewer columns, and they are either completely or nearly independent from each other. That lack of correlation enables the next step, segmentation using traditional *cluster analysis*. Cluster analysis groups together data points (in this case, consumers) that are close to each other by geometric distance There are different approaches to cluster analysis, based on alternative distance metrics and algorithms, more details of these may be found in Duda, Hart and Stork (2001). A critical step in cluster analysis is determining the number of clusters. This is determined based on the cluster algorithms, as well as business criteria. Typically clustering for a market exercise aims to yield between three and eight groups, and these groups become known as the segments.

After the segments are created, they have to be interpreted in relevant business meaning and impact. Can we assign a name to each cluster? Can we describe them in a few short sentences? What are the ways to communicate with this group, and what behaviors of this segment do want to change? These are litmus tests of whether our segmentation exercise has been valuable.

SECONDARY DATA SOURCES FOR SEGMENTATION

As an alternative method for quantitative segmentation, existing secondary datasets may be consulted. Demographic information can come from public sources such as the US Census Bureau, which provides counts of populations by age, gender, and geography. Also worth exploring are household-level psychographics datasets such as Personicx, which can overlay demographics with purchasing behaviors and media consumption.

Another source for consumer segmentation in pharmaceuticals are the patient-level longitudinal claims datasets, which can categorize patients within a therapeutic category by their prescription behavior. Segments that may come out of such claims data include:

- patients newly treating within a category;

- patients switching between therapies;

- patients treating primarily with generics.

Demographic data such as age, gender, and geography can be overlaid with these patient-level data sets as well. However, note that untreated patients, or those not treating with pharmaceuticals, will not be included.

PRIORITIZING AND TARGETING THE SEGMENTS

Once a modest number of meaningful segments have been determined, they need to be prioritized as to which should be the targets of a CRM program. Figure 4.3 illustrates a framework as to how one can prioritize. Segments should be considered based on size (number of members), as well as based on the potential Rx impact (monetized as accurately as possible) that CRM could have per member of this segment. With these factors in mind, we can suggest preliminary decisions on segments:

- *High volume, high potential impact*: these are the prime targets for CRM. For example, consider the smoking cessation category, and the segment of consumers who are motivated to quit but need help with the right medication, devices, and behavior modification programs.

- *Low volume, low potential impact*: these segments should be excluded from CRM planning. For example, patients who are already adherent and managing their disease successfully with a competitive medication. They are unlikely to be swayed by a CRM program of an alternative drug.

- *High volume, low potential impact*: these segments could be a financial expense for a marketing organization, with minimal

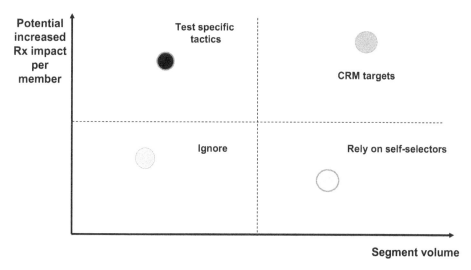

Figure 4.3   Prioritizing segments for consumer relationship marketing

payoff. For example, in cardiovascular categories like hypertension or hyperlipidemia, some patients are "naturalists," eschewing medication, and feeling that they can address their problems exclusively with diet and exercise. For such patients, it will be challenging to change their point of view entirely. However, a company can offer a CRM program consistent with their viewpoint, such as medication with natural diet and exercise tips and guidelines. With such a nuanced CRM program, the company can expect a small percentage of "self-selectors" from this segment to choose that CRM offering, and the medication as well.

- *Low volume, high potential impact*: these segments can bring high payoff of CRM, but some tailoring of tactics or channels may be required specific to this segment. One classic example here is patients new to a medication who require persistence and compliance programs to stay on that medication. Another example is those who are highly motivated but may need copay assistance to get over financial hurdles. These CRM program components are worth developing, but should be continually tested and evaluated for effectiveness.

Professional Segmentation For Relationship Marketing

Professional Relationship Marketing (PRM) must be designed with a business strategy in mind that goes beyond the basic drug product message. Developing that strategy helps a pharmaceutical company plan appropriate promotional channels, in-market tactics, and tailored messages to reach their valuable professional customers.

The strategy starts with understanding the HCP segments appropriate to the therapeutic categories in question. The dimensions of segmentation include:

- treatment patterns (prescription writing, speed to adoption of new products, brand loyalty versus "spreading");

- office practice objectives (growing patient base, training staff, reducing administrative burden, forming a group or network);

- preferred promotional consumption mix (sales representatives, websites, mobile, print, conventions).

Some of these segments can be determined from large-scale secondary data analysis. Further clarity of the segmentation may be filled in from brief primary surveys of professionals.

As an example of how HCP segmentation can play a critical role in go-to-market strategy, consider a pharmaceutical company making preparations to launch a new product that is predicted to be successful but nowhere near blockbuster (billion dollar annual sales) level. The pharmaceutical company has a primary strategic objective of spreading early awareness and product trial among physicians. After that trial, the goal is for early adopting professionals (and patients) to share their experiences and then to accelerate the launch uptake curve. However, as a challenge of this case, the company can only commit a limited number of sales representatives to this launch. Therefore, there is an additional goal of determining the right mix of promotional versus non-personal promotion.

In order to assist in this prioritization, we can rely on segmentation based on three primary dimensions, as illustrated in Figure 4.4:

1. *Prescribing volume* within the therapeutic category, over a recent time period. A standard decile approach can be used where physicians are assigned values from 1 (highest) to 10 (lowest) using prescriber-level retail prescription data. There are nuances to decile assignment. Often, non-prescribers are filtered out, or given a decile score of zero. For the remaining actual prescribers, scores of 1 to 10 can be given so that there are either equal numbers of physicians within each category, or an equal number of prescriptions within each category. In the former case, decile 1 will, by definition, include exactly 10 percent of the prescribers, and in the latter case, fewer prescribers will be at the highest values, and decile 1 will include far fewer than 10 percent of prescribers.

2. *Historical speed to new drug adoption* based on previous prescribing of new drugs launched in recent years in related therapeutic categories. The terms "recent" and "related" give latitude to companies to make selections best suited to their needs. For example, recent may mean three to five years, and examples of related therapeutic categories

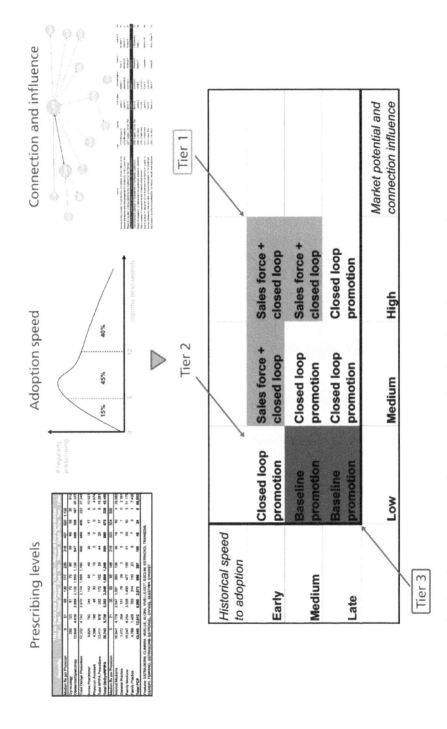

Figure 4.4   Professional segmentation for a new product launch assists go-to-market strategy

are chronic cardiovascular categories such as hypertension, hyperlipidemia, and diabetes. Previous analyses within chronic retail-based prescription categories suggests that up to 10 percent to 20 percent of category prescribers have a historical tendency for adoption of new products within the first six months. Note also that specialists tend to be earlier adopters of new medications, based on their exposure to more challenging patients and their frequent exposure to innovative research at journals and conferences. Of course, early adoption results would vary by therapeutic category and by how many prescriptions one considers at an adoption level.

3.   *Connection and influence* indicators can be assigned to HCPs based on whether their reputations and opinions may be influential toward spreading trial and adoption of the new medication. The top right of Figure 4.4 shows a connection network between professionals, from which it can be inferred who the highly connected professionals are: those with many connection links emanating from their graph node. A linkage between two professionals can be based on any one of several criteria:

   •   joint publication of articles from a health library resource like PubMed;

   •   joint participation on clinical trials within the relevant therapeutic category, as determined by listings from public registries like ClinicalTrials.gov;

   •   self-reported statements of influence, or value of opinion, from primary market research;

   •   referral connections, where many primary care physicians are referring to a common specialist.

Using these three dimensions, one can develop a strategy of which promotional channels to assign to which professionals, and this is illustrated in the lower part of Figure 4.4.

   •   Tier 1 professionals (green) are early to medium adopters and early to medium prescribing volume. Also included in Tier 1 are the highly connected influencers.

- Tier 2 professionals (yellow) are low to medium in either adoption speed or in prescribing, but not both.

- Tier 3 professionals (red) are the late adopters and the low to medium prescribing volumes

Using this tiered segmentation, if specific numbers are assigned to each tier, then we can potentially estimate the number of sales representatives required. For instance, say Tier 1 totals 10,000 professionals. Then, the number of sales representatives to cover phase 1 can be estimated from their expected monthly reach. A monthly reach of 80 yields 125 representatives, while a monthly reach of 100 yields 100 representatives.

In the following chapter, we shall develop a distinctive RM experience for each of the professional segments we have described.

Personas and Experiences by Segment

Once the target segments for CRM or PRM are determined, a critical next step is developing a strategy and contact plan for each of these segments. An excellent way to achieve this is via *personas*. A persona is a prototype of a consumer or professional belonging to a targeted segment, fully fleshed out with demographics, attitudes, life experiences, healthcare treatments, and media channel preferences.

CONSUMER (PATIENT) PERSONAS

As an example, let's consider a persona for the fibromyalgia category, illustrated in Figure 4.5. One critical segment for CRM are patients who have long suffered with chronic, widespread pain, and are newly diagnosed with fibromyalgia. Market research has shown the target demographic of this segment are middle-aged women, many of whom have careers that they have had to compromise as a result of their pain. In the figure we have created a persona named Linda who embodies these research findings. Linda is a 48-year-old university professor from Oregon, with a photograph as an illustration (from stock photography).

Beyond these demographic figures, there is also an *experience map* of the healthcare journey Linda has had so far. An experience map is a sequence of significant milestones that personas engage in to illustrate the strategy required

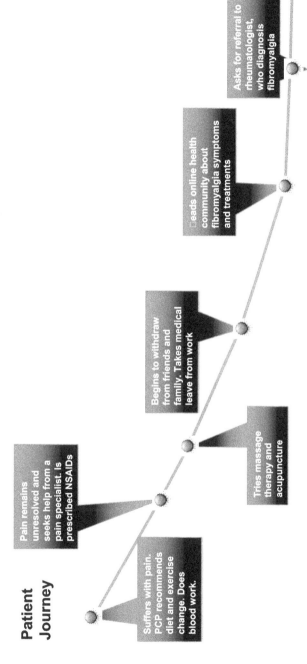

Name: Linda **Segment:** Newly diagnosed

Gender: Female **Age:** 48

Occupation: Fine Arts Professor at a University

Hometown: Eugene, Oregon

Patient Journey

Suffers with pain. PCP recommends diet and exercise change. Does blood work.

Pain remains unresolved and seeks help from a pain specialist. Is prescribed NSAIDs

Tries massage therapy and acupuncture

Begins to withdraw from friends and family. Takes medical leave from work

Reads online health community about fibromyalgia symptoms and treatments

Asks for referral to rheumatologist, who diagnosis fibromyalgia

Figure 4.5 Persona of a target consumer segment, fibromyalgia category

for a RM program. In this case, the experience map starts when Linda was told by her primary care physician to improve her diet and exercise more, which she did but saw no improvement in pain. Linda subsequently tried alternative treatments like acupuncture and message therapy. Over time, Linda had to take leave from work, and reduce time with friends and family, as it was difficult to cope with her pain in social settings. She eventually read about fibromyalgia on the Internet within social network communities, and learned of other people, strangers to her, who sought treatment with a rheumatologist. Armed with this background, Linda asked her primary care physician for a referral to a rheumatologist, and soon thereafter was diagnosed properly with fibromyalgia. This journey, in fact, has taken years to develop.

As shown by this description, some liberties can be taken with personas to fully flesh out a character. In this case, Linda's department of study and city of residence, and even race, are not critical. However, these embellishments make marketing strategists feel they are addressing the healthcare needs of actual people.

The experience we have just illustrated is for a persona where the patient is becoming diagnosed and seeking treatment. It is also necessary to map out an experience related to patient conversion to therapy and adherence. Figure 4.6 shows such an experience based on our exercises at the end of each chapter for the fictitious ABC Pharmaceuticals and the soon-to-launch osteoporosis therapy called ABCOS. In this case the persona is a 61-year-old female patient named Martha. The figure illustrates how Martha searches online for osteoporosis, is directed to the ABCOS website, and reads in-depth information. Then Martha takes a branded discussion guide to her physician and receives a prescription for the monthly treatment ABCOS. There is a copay reduction offer for the first treatment, which is tied to enrollment within an adherence program. Martha makes use of the tracking tools within the adherence program, answers survey questions, and utilizes a self-tracking diary on her mobility and pain relief while on ABCOS. She shares the results of the self-tracking with her physician at follow up visits.

The benefit of this particular patient experience is that it illustrates several vital components of a CRM program: media channels, website design, registration, value exchange, and continuing progress. It spells out a template on which ABC Pharmaceuticals can measure progress when actual patients are interacting with these in-market CRM tactics.

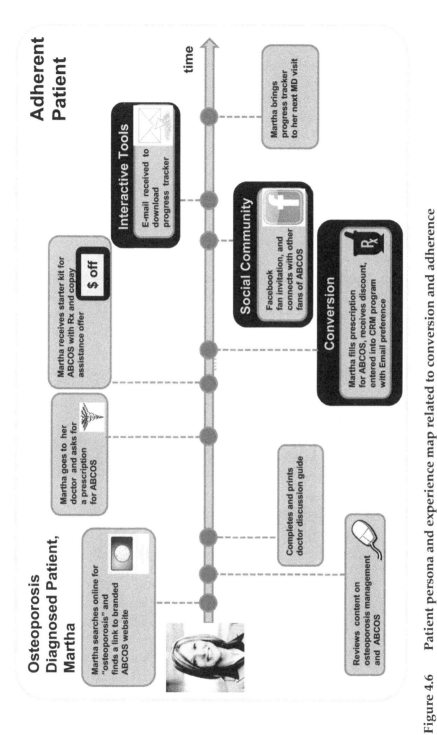

Figure 4.6   Patient persona and experience map related to conversion and adherence

When planning strategies for pharmaceutical CRM, at least one persona is typically mapped out for each of the key targeted segments. The benefits of personas are they bring a segment to life, enable discussions about marketing strategies, and guide development of specific tactics. However, one must also realize that the thousands of members within a segment are not identical to this persona. The segment members in fact have variations that could require nuances of marketplace tactics.

PERSONAS FOR PROFESSIONALS AND SALES REPRESENTATIVES

Similarly, personas and experience maps can also be developed for PRM. For PRM, not only do we develop a persona for the HCPs that are the target for our program, but also the sales representatives that are calling on those professionals. To illustrate these personas, please see Figure 4.7, which illustrates the persona of a Dr Sam Johnson, a Tier 1 primary care physician in Chicago who, due to his high patient volume, is called on by multiple pharmaceutical sales representatives. One of these is represented in the persona of Amber McKeown, a representative in the Chicago territory from ABC Pharmaceuticals, manufacturer of ABCOS from our homework exercises. Further embellishments could be given to each of these personas regarding demographics, attitudes, or behaviors, if necessary.

One benefit of PRM is that it can enable true "value based selling" where a pharmaceutical company can listen to a physician's clinical and practice needs, and respond appropriately. Physician value can be actually be enhanced and measured through deployment of a PRM system offering a range of services that go with the product information. Furthermore, through online surveys and click stream data from registrants, professional goals can be better assessed, and even brought back to the healthcare company or the sales representative in a feedback loop. On these company portfolio portals, HCPs can find practice resources as well as product information. In turn, healthcare companies can measure, gather feedback, and be more responsive over time.

The experience map illustrated in Figure 4.7 shows the planned interactions that Dr Johnson would have with Amber McKeown, as it relates to a designed ABC portfolio PRM system with a feedback loop. First, Dr Johnson sees an online banner advertisement for the ABC Pharmaceuticals portfolio PRM website within an online physician portal (such as WebMD). He does not click through immediately. Within a week, on her next call to visit Dr Johnson, Amber McKeown mentions the PRM website and the series of product information

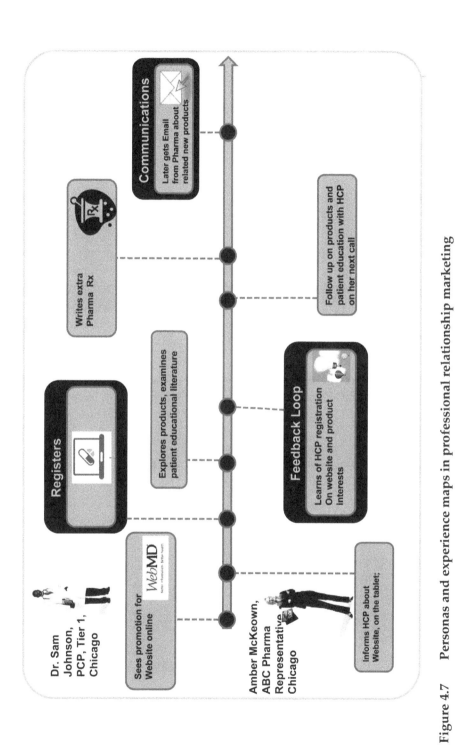

Figure 4.7   Personas and experience maps in professional relationship marketing

and professional services that are available to registered participants. Shortly thereafter, Dr Johnson registers on the website and explores ABC products, and also downloads patient educational materials in the area of menopausal health.

The feedback loop of the PRM system forms the next part of this experience map. Amber learns via her contact management system that Dr Johnson has registered for the ABC PRM portal and what types of activities he has explored. This helps Amber plan her next visit to Dr Johnson, in which she mentions particular products that Dr Johnson has reviewed, and points out the range of patient literature and resources that ABC Pharmaceuticals can make available to Dr Johnson's practice. Dr Johnson notices and appreciates this extra level of responsiveness by ABC Pharmaceuticals and Amber. In the longer term, Dr Johnson may increase his prescribing of ABC products, knowing that there is always valuable information and support for his patients along with those prescribed medications. In addition, because Dr Johnson has registered on the PRM website, he receives emails about upcoming ABC Pharmaceuticals events at conventions and invitations to webinars from key opinion leaders (KOLs) in the area of menopausal health.

This experience map serves as not only an illustration but also a target case for what the actual PRM system should be able to achieve. It can be revisited as progress is made during a phased approach to PRM development.

Developing a Strategic Insight for Consumer Relationship Marketing Campaigns

With the consumer segments prioritized and embodied within personas, marketers still have the challenge of determining what exactly will motivate consumers to take action at critical points of their patient journey. For example, what will drive an undiagnosed patient into the doctor's office to get a proper diagnosis and treatment? Alternatively, what motivates a patient who is just given a prescription medication to stay on therapy? The driving factors may be wide ranging and include:

- *fear* of the unknown, future illness, or death;

- *empathy* with other role models or celebrities depicted in advertising;

- *aspirations*, to attain certain goals, or live to certain milestones (such as a child's wedding);

- *rewards*, such as improved quality of life, or even financial incentives.

In fact, these motivational factors may differ by segment.

To gather an expert opinion on the role of strategic insight for pharmaceutical CRM campaigns, we have interviewed Jennifer Matthews, Partner at the healthcare communications agency The CementBloc, and formerly Senior Vice President and leader of the healthcare practice at Wunderman.

Haimowitz: What is the role of strategic insights within Pharmaceutical CRM?

Matthews: The role is foundational. Landing on the right set of insights, and identifying a core insight that encapsulates what will be most motivational to consumers is critical. The strategic insights then inform a creative execution that connects to patients and motivates those patients to engage with the CRM program.

Haimowitz: What is the best process for coming up with strategic insights for a CRM campaign?

Matthews: We employ a variety of research methods, including looking at market data, understanding treatment algorithims and paradigms, all with an effort to understand the situation the patient is in. But getting at deep insights requires speaking to and interacting with patients. This begins with a healthy amount of primary qualitative research to tease out the motivators that drive or bar action. CRM is about taking action, so that consumers will engage with the brand. What's challenging in healthcare is that attitudes and behaviors don't necessarily align. People may know what they should do to maintain their health, to eat right and exercise, especially those suffering from chronic disease. Yet so often, the opposite occurs. Patients know they should be doing one thing, yet behave another way. We often recommend interviewing the patients in their home environment as well as in the clinical setting. This affords an opportunity to better understand the impact of the condition on their lifestyle and loved ones as well as the dynamics between patients and healthcare providers. A qualitative approach that includes ethnographies and in-office visit monitoring can help to uncover the insights that can form the basis of the program.

Haimowitz: What is more challenging in healthcare relationship marketing as compared to other industries?

Matthews: Healthcare is challenging given the knowledge that people should do better. Consider adherence. Even with life saving or life-enhancing medications, typical adherence curves show dramatic drop off between three and five months, whether it be oncology or cholesterol medication. There is a recognition that we should be doing better than this. There is much irrational behavior; patients know they should be taking these medications, yet they do not act logically. Behaviors are deeply ingrained. The challenge for us is to understand how we can move the needle. What content, tools, offers can we provide that will affect that behavior? How can we construct an engagement platform that can provide meaningful education resulting in action?

Haimowitz: How does the CRM strategy incorporate a product's brand positioning?

Matthews: CRM activates the brand strategy by aligning it to an engagement strategy for patients. The positioning of the brand is central to CRM, in that it encapsulates the brand strategy. From an executional perspective, CRM content may be unbranded or branded, but all of it must align back to the positioning of the brand. Further "upstream," for awareness, the content may skew to unbranded disease education. For acquisition, brand attributes and benefits are introduced.

This is especially valuable for patients who are already educated on the disease or condition, and now want find out information on specific products, either because they have been prescribed that medication, or they are considering a switch from one medication to another. For adherence, the content may focus on side-effect management, medication reminders, and financial support.

Haimowitz: Can you please give an example of where the right CRM campaign strategy can really make a demonstrable impact in pharmaceutical CRM?

Matthews: Consider the smoking cessation category, which is broad and consists of over-the-counter products, prescription alternatives, hypnosis, and homeopathic remedies, and of course "cold turkey." All of these options share a common challenge: low chance of success. And this is compounded by the fact that patients are rarely successful. Ninety-seven percent of smokers try to quit, yet only 3 percent succeed. It takes an average of seven quit attempts to actually succeed. So, we are up against low expectations. Smokers have been conditioned to believe that the low rate of quitting is based on weak willpower and that it's just a bad habit than can be broken. The objective, of course, is to improve the success rates. The way to achieve this is to prompt patients to think differently about quitting and to shift the conversation away from willpower. In the CRM campaign I supported for a major manufacturer, we created an unbranded educational platform that "medicalized" smoking cessation by transferring the blame from the individual to the real issue: nicotine addiction. In creating the program, we embraced the principles of behavior modification, built upon the Stages of Change Model by Dr Prochaska (see Prochaska, Norcross, and DiClemente 1994). We also included a decisional balance tool, which was a central component of a segmentation strategy determining whether a patient was truly ready to quit. This was so critical for brand success, as we did not want to attract smokers who weren't in the appropriate frame of mind to succeed in their quit attempt. The category is littered with products that have overstated efficacy and the notion of "magic pill" is one we needed to clearly avoid.

Haimowitz: How can one test whether the CRM campaign strategy is sound?

Matthews: Typically after a round of qualitative and perhaps quantitative insight mining research, we construct a CRM value proposition and associated core assets to the program itself, that may be services, content, tools and/or offers. Then we conduct follow-on market research to determine if the value proposition is relevant, meaningful and above all, motivating to our patients. Through this research, we hone and improve the program proposition and assets, ensuring relevance to patients and healthcare providers, including physicians, nurses and/or allied health professionals. Once research is complete, the creative expression of the campaign can be developed. Of course, another way to validate the CRM strategy is to measure the in-market performance of an executed campaign, after it is developed. This measurement takes place by tracking consumer attitudes of those enrolled versus a control group, benchmarking opt-in and also using anonymous longitudinal claims data to measure incremental medication conversion or adherence.

Haimowitz: Are there any particular future trends that you see within CRM?

Matthews: I see three major trends: First, what is becoming clear is that the definition of "CRM" is changing, in that the communication is no longer restricted to segmented, outbound communications sent by pharmaceutical companies to patients opting-in and signing up in a database. Now, with the advent of mobile communications and social media, CRM is becoming more customized to how patients are seeking information, and interacting with healthcare content overall. Now patients can self-identify and access segmented health information online, even if they do not explicitly opt-in and answer a survey about themselves. Via the Internet, patients can find customized, segmented information on therapy management and disease state management that is dynamically served. Second, some pharmaceutical companies used to think of CRM as primarily about compliance and persistency, but many now understand CRM strategy applies across the patient continuum, from pre-diagnosis through advocacy. Overall, CRM is becoming less brand-centric and more customer-centric. And manufacturers are seeking CRM solutions across portfolios of products. Third, more and more, we are seeing manufacturers apply the fundamental principles of CRM to their HCP go-to-market strategies. Segmenting their professional customers based on attitudes, needs, and preferences in addition to their Rx writing value, helps marketers better understand how to engage with these customers. The integration of personal and non-personal selling, through an intelligent, data-based feedback loop represents the convergence of sales and marketing.

Media Planning and Selection

MEDIA PLANNING FOR CONSUMER RELATIONSHIP MARKETING

A critical element of CRM is selecting media tailored to the CRM segments, at the moment they are making critical healthcare decisions. The segmentation and personas are valuable starting points for this media planning. Consider again the persona of Linda from Figure 4.5. The critical point in Linda's patient journey (see beginning of this chapter) we are trying to influence is her seeing a specialist to get properly diagnosed.

We will touch on the basics of media planning; a more detailed treatment can be found in specialty texts on media planning such as Baron and Sissors (2010). We need to think about how to reach Linda's demographic to help determine her media consumption habits. First note that as an American woman in her 40s, Linda is a likely consumer of certain magazines, cable television channels, and Internet websites. In fact, specialized data sources can help provide detailed information on consumer's media consumption habits.

Simmons data provides television, magazine, and sporting event consumption habits by demographics. *Commscore data* provides Internet website consumption habits by demographics.

In addition, we need to consider Linda's medical history and what type of information she may be seeking. As a longtime pain sufferer, Linda may be searching for answers online as to how to manage her pain. She may be visiting pain-related website content on healthcare portals (such as WebMD, Yahoo Health, or HealthCentral), as well as joining online communities related to pain management.

Typically, the goal of advertising for CRM is to elicit a *direct response (DR),* meaning that viewers of the advertisement are encouraged to take action via phone, mail, or the Internet. This contrasts with *general awareness* (GA) advertising, where the primary objective is to communicate product branding. See Table 4.2 below for crucial differences between GA and DR advertising.

As shown in the table, GA advertising employs mass media and broadcast channels to spread awareness of the brand name and product attributes. By contrast, DR advertising employs targeted media and communicates offers and incentives to consumers, listing specific response channels where consumers can act, such as mail, toll-free numbers, and website addresses. Accordingly, the success metrics differ for the two classes of advertising. GA advertising measures success based on the reach of consumers that view the advertisement, as well as the average frequency of the advertising seen. Reach and frequency are combined together using metrics like circulation, impressions, and gross rating points (GRPs). A GRP is an index based on 100 that gives the percentage of the target audience viewing the advertising during a time period and over a channel. Efficiency of GA advertising can be viewed in cost per thousand impressions (CPM). After the advertising has run, success is measured by consumer-reported brand awareness and message awareness. Direct response advertising, more relevant to CRM, measures success by responders, or leads, who take action as a result of the advertisement. Efficiency is measured in the cost per lead (CPL), or more specifically cost per qualified lead (CPQL), where a qualified lead registers for the RM program and also belongs to the target segment.

When planning media purchase, and weighing broadcast versus targeted media channels, one must realize this is not a clear distinction, but rather a spectrum, which is illustrated in Figure 4.8.

Table 4.2   Differences between general awareness and direct response advertising

	General Awareness Advertising	Direct Response Advertising
Media channels	Broadcast, mass media	Targeted media
Messages	Product attributes, brand name	Offers, incentives, response mechanisms
Success metrics	Reach, frequency, gross rating points, impressions, brand/message awareness	Responders (leads), cost per lead, cost per qualified lead

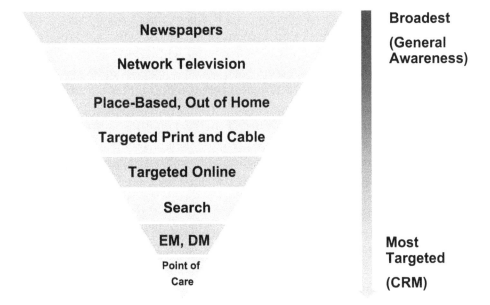

Figure 4.8   Consumer media planning channels for CRM

At the top of the figure are broadcast channels reaching wide audiences, such as newspapers and network television. Toward the bottom of the figure are the most targeted channels, which aim to reach consumers when and where they are most likely to be at a critical decision moment. Included in these are:

- *Targeted print and cable television*: these are magazines and television stations that are specific to certain subpopulations. Some are geared toward particular demographics, in the way that *Oxygen* and *Lifetime* television as well as *More* and *Good Housekeeping* magazines are geared toward middle-aged women. Others are specialized by medical condition, like *Arthritis Today* or *Cure*.

- *Targeted online placements*: quite similar to print and cable, there are plenty of online portals and communities geared toward specific demographics. Not only are there reproductions online of nearly all specialized magazines, but there are also online communities specific to demographics. Consider new mothers: www.babycenter.com is one of many online communities with large followings accepting advertising. Similarly, most online health portals such as webmd.com, health.yahoo.com and revolutionhealth.com have specialized content areas that accept focused advertising.

- *Direct mail and email*: list vendors including publishers and other consumer information collectors will rent the right to postal mail or email individuals or households having people with particular medical conditions, or even taking particular medications. While these may appear targeted, one should be cautious as information may not be up to date, and response rates may vary widely. More on direct response rates in Chapter 5.

- *Search engine marketing*: a consumer search is an expression of interest or intent related to some topic or product. Thus, responses to searches are a chance to engage a consumer that is already partway down the patient journey. Paid search advertising remains a viable online media option, even after additional restrictions were placed by the US Food and Drug Administration (FDA) on paid search advertising in 2009. Leading search engines at the time of writing include Google, Yahoo, Bing, and Ask. In addition to advertising with paid search, it behooves online marketers to invest time on search engine optimization, perform a thorough keyword tagging of website pages to get one's website highly referenced and indexed. This will lead to improved search engine rankings as well.

- *Point of care promotion*: while not exactly media outlets, physician's offices and clinics can be quite effective in reaching targeted consumers with particular conditions at the diagnosis or treatment stage of the patient treatment continuum. Point of care promotional tactics include:

  - in-office patient brochures on unbranded health topics or specific brands;

  - health-related "cover wraps" on waiting room magazines;

-   screening questionnaires asking patients if they might have a condition;

-   registration tablets (whether paper, or electronic like Phreesia);

-   discount offers within drug starter kits.

When developing a media plan for CRM direct response, all of the options in Figure 4.8 may be available, depending on the promotional budget. Given that budget, a media plan can be developed that reaches the appropriate targets, at the right stage of the patient treatment continuum. The goal is to cover a certain reach and impression/circulation level, while optimizing cost per qualified lead. Benchmark books from the Direct Marketing Association (see www.the-dma.org) is a good place to obtain response rate guidelines.

A media plan is often designed to cover a calendar year, and laid out in a diagram much like Figure 4.9. Each media channel is given a row, and columns are shaded at the right for each month of the year where that channel is purchased. The shaded cells can also be filled in with other quantitative data, like the number of GRPs, the number of impressions, or dollars spent that month. Other data not fitting here will appear in supplemental spreadsheets. The benefit of a media plan layout, such as that shown in Figure 4.9, is seeing all media channels together, aligned with the calendar, and other marketplace events. Another benefit is assistance with design of experiments, a subject we will examine in the next chapter.

MEDIA PLANNING FOR PROFESSIONAL RELATIONSHIP MARKETING

For professionals, typically RM media planning is more straightforward, and includes finding venues where professionals are likely to be engaged in seeking information within the therapeutic category of the RM program. These venues include:

-   medical conventions, and the literature, signage, and tradeshow booths associated with these;

-   targeted publications, both print and electronic;

-   targeted professional website portals containing medical content of the appropriate therapeutic classes.

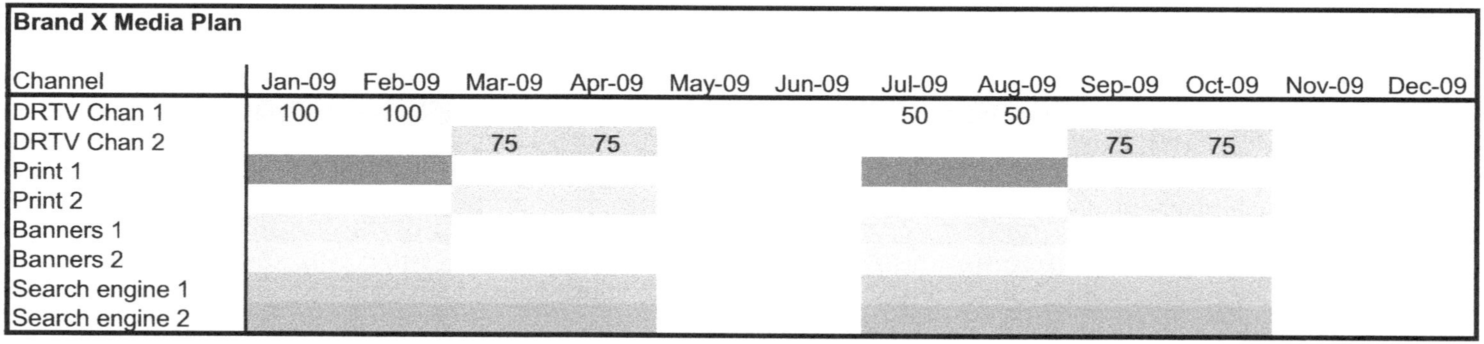

Figure 4.9 Annual layout of a media plan

As with consumer media planning, media selections are made based on the goals of motivating professionals along their journey. This dictates the relative weight of awareness versus direct response. For a given high impression total, those tactics with highest expected response rates are selected.

Creative and Message Development

Once a CRM campaign has developed its target segments, as well as its strategic insights, then planning begins for creative development. Creative development consists of everything that consumers can sense, and is a combination of images, audio, video, and text copy, within some particular media channel or on a mobile device. When considering creative development and CRM, crucial components include:

- *striking imagery* that is eye-catching and cuts through the clutter of the crowded promotional landscape;

- a *relevant message* that consumers can relate to and that speaks to that consumer's place in the aforementioned treatment continuum;

- a *value exchange* that enumerates what the consumer will receive in exchange for signing up for the RM program;

- a *call to action* for the consumer to respond, with an associated offer or incentive.

For professional RM, these four elements also need to be in place. One notable clarification for PRM is that the message and the value exchange are most relevant for professionals when they appeal to their business objectives: such as services for practice management, educating patients, training staff, and so on.

To gain an expert opinion on the benefit of creative and messaging to RM, especially for consumers, we have interviewed Elizabeth Elfenbein, Partner at the healthcare advertising agency The CementBloc, and formerly Creative Director at the prestigious RM agency, Wunderman.

Haimowitz: What is the role of strong creative in activating consumers and patients within pharmaceutical CRM?

Elfenbein: What is really important with strong creative is the ability to really connect and understand what patients are going through. When you look at CRM, this is about having a relationship over an illness, a product lifecycle, or even a lifetime. Unless you are empathetic and understanding, patients will not take having a relationship seriously. So, you have to understand what it's like to live in their skin, understand their plight and walk in their shoes. A lot of these illnesses are chronic and can last for years, so it's about understanding the patients' journey in order to keep them motivated and ensure they take their medicine.

Creative is really important because if it does it's job, its connecting with the key insights to what patients are really going through. I feel like you cannot quantify someone's feelings but you can qualify them. Good creative often qualifies those feelings, including the patient's struggles.

Also important to effective CRM creative is the notion of understanding the universal truths, and also the differences among populations. Good creative must really connect across those differences; otherwise the resulting communication may be too topical and generic. For example, if oncology communications feature "beaches," patients may feel, "that is not me, I have cancer," and this creative will not connect on an emotional level.

Haimowitz: You spoke about "universal truths," can you please clarify what you mean?

Elfenbein: Well, when a CRM strategy team goes through research, and when an agency puts a creative brief out, there are insights, and in addition many creative professionals research further on their own. They seek to find out: what are common "universal truths" and what are the universal differences, and where do they intersect, the truths and the differences.

For example, for patients with metastatic breast cancer, they have been poked and prodded for long periods of time and they are sick of being sick, and just want to be treated like individuals. These patients often feel devalued, this is a universal truth. They feel like a scientific, medical experiment. The truth in this is that even though patients express this differently, they all express this sentiment of feeling devalued. The universal difference is they all are unique, independent human beings, and all have different approaches to life. They are themselves first; they are happy to undergo the treatment, but still want to maintain their identity. So their differences are what identify them as a person, and what is common is the shared experience like the illness. Milestones in people's lives are universal truths, those are topics that most can identify with, and patients can also identify with some of their feelings, and that makes the communication become very personal.

Haimowitz: How would you weigh the specific contributions of creative elements like images, layout, copy, messaging, offers, and calls to action?

Elfenbein: The first thing is to get the "big idea"—the image and the copy, how they intersect and how they fit together. The goal is to juxtapose a very strong image with the right copy. The concept has to draw you in; it needs to have stopping power, and it has to feel different. The concept has to compete in this world, where there is a ton of clutter, and very little whitespace. You are competing on so many levels, not only with pharmaceuticals, but also with consumer packaged goods. So emotional stopping power is critical.

Then from an insights perspective, there must be a connection to consumers. People have to see materials and say, "that's me," meaning they can see themselves and identify with it. Layout is important because even with a great image and great copy, it's really about "dominant and subdominant." So, if your image is the "hero," what is important is how the image and the layout are combined so that they work together. Those with a sense of design understand that both cannot be dominant.

When you look at messaging, incentives, and call to action, first if you do not have an image with stopping power, all of that is irrelevant. But how fantastic it is when the story is told and there is clarity on what the patient should do. The goal is to connect with patients, and drive a certain behavior and call to action. For example, in the category of smoking cessation, it has been successful to have patients identify with the struggle to quit smoking, and see it as their personal journey. "Let's get real," an "AHA moment," when a smoker gets that smoking isn't just a habit, it's an addiction. Then, that connection is supplemented with the action those patients should take, in this case, to find out more information and create a plan to quit.

In RM, it's about very singularly driving that behavior. If there is too much copy, or the wrong kind of non-emotional copy, you are not going to make a connection and then the CRM will not drive that behavior.

Haimowitz: Have you seen the right "big idea" make a genuine difference in pharmaceutical CRM outcomes, such as prescription levels, or financial impact?

Elfenbein: Yes, I have seen this in several categories, including allergies, breast cancer, and smoking cessation. The allergy marketplace is very saturated with so many products that are over-the-counter. Therefore incentives made sense and played a prominent role. Also, because of seasonality of allergies, we offered a program built around that seasonality and encouraged filling prescriptions, that yielded great results. With breast cancer, there is a different way to make an impact. For example, we have worked on a (non-hormonal) product with dosing along a five year continuum, and we noticed a persistence curve decline at certain time periods even within the first year. Therefore we created materials to address the time periods to get people to stay on therapy. We aimed to address the specific barriers patients have at each time, and were able to improve the persistence pattern for CRM participants.

For smoking cessation, this was a very challenging category requiring innovative therapies, and we were involved in a product launch requiring lead generation with a combination of unbranded and branded campaigns. We also found that this was about timing. A seamless 360-degree experience encouraging registration and following up with unbranded and branded fulfillment, as appropriate. Then following up directly with registered consumers, to make sure patients were sticking to their "quit plan." Critical to success was understanding the psychology of quitting smoking during the days and weeks ahead, as well as the physical feelings of a smoker quitting cigarettes, and pairing up the communication materials to address the patients' physical feelings. For example, reinforcing positive behaviors of quitting smoking for several weeks by utilizing a game with rewards.

Haimowitz: What kind of testing is done on creative for CRM? What are the relative benefits of pre-testing versus in-market testing of alternative creative executions?

Elfenbein: We do extensive primary research testing and focus groups, going around the country, to different regions and cities, including one-on-ones as well as groups of consumers. Testing is done on different segments, and various ethnicities. During the research we put three to five ideas in front of consumers, some of these shocking, and here is where you see the universal truths. For example, in smoking cessation, I saw a 70-year-old retired military man who felt the same as several middle-aged women about their struggles to quit. The struggle was universal, and you aim to connect with most of the group.

Research from an online perspective can enable more quantitative results. You can put up a storyboard or a prototype website online and get a larger volume of responses to it. What is required regardless of the methodology is creating an ad-like object, or "adlob" for consumers to react to. It is difficult to evaluate creative or messaging without an adlob. We sometimes conduct quantitative research with messaging, although this can be somewhat unreliable, because consumers at times just go with their gut instincts in responding to alternative messages.

Haimowitz: Is there anything else you would like to add about the role of creative in RM?

Elfenbein: We are developing a new approach to developing creative for RM, a philosophy where there is a science, left brain versus right brain, emotional and rational. When you look at the brand ladder, with functional at bottom and emotional at the top, it is critical to determine what is right for both the "customer" and the brand. This customer can be patient or a physician.

You can get a lot of range when you develop creative work using this approach, it's also important to realize that creative work is always a testable proposition. Sometimes with multiple strong options, it is best to let customers decide what connects with them. The goal is to develop work that connects and changes behavior, not just work that aims to be clever. We need to be clever, however, more importantly, we must demonstrate to our customers that we understand their struggles, their successes; every step that helps them be who they are. We believe that when we demonstrate this, it will result in behaviors that help drive Rx and business sales.

One final point I'd like to make relates specifically to digital channels. Consumers now use the Internet extensively for health information and trust it more than their doctor. As we develop CRM communications, this challenges us: how can we create the right content for people online? How can we insert ourselves into their lives and provide the best brand experience across all channels that will drive behavior?

Exercises for Chapter 4

We return to our running case study of ABC Pharmaceuticals and the pre-launch osteoporosis treatment ABCOS, which will be a once-monthly non-oral. Consider these questions related to develop a strategy for the eventual CRM program:

Question 4.1 What market research with consumers can be designed for developing a strategy around the launch of the ABCOS CRM program?

Question 4.2 What media channels might be appropriate for the target osteoporosis patients who would take ABCOS?

Question 4.3 How could creative elements of the CRM program demonstrate empathy for the osteoporosis patients who would take ABCOS?

Analytics Planning for Relationship Marketing

In the previous chapter we outlined most of the primary components of the strategy behind a healthcare relationship marketing (RM) program. We have separated out the strategic development that is related to analytics. This chapter enumerates a series of steps a designer of consumer relationship marketing (CRM) or professional relationship marketing (PRM) programs should consider to insure that this program can be measured and continually optimized.

Measuring Versus Goals: The Relationship Marketing Learning Plan

Before deployment of a pharmaceutical RM program, one has to design a blueprint of how the program will be measured, and under what conditions adjustments need to be made. This truism holds across industries and all types of promotional campaigns: *Measurement is most valuable when it is aligned with the promotion's business objectives.* While this statement may seem obvious, this has implications that are often overlooked:

- One should develop campaign tactics (channels, communications) that are in-line with the marketing brand's business objectives. Occasionally marketers will jump immediately into trial tactics like social media, or patient support programs, without considering the overall business goals of these tactics.

- One should obtain measurements that can help prove or disprove that the brand's business objectives are in fact being met. Without advance planning, one may mistakenly measure inconsequential data, like website visits or page views, rather than visits that are qualified acquired leads.

The blueprint to what shall be measured, with implications for decision making, is called a *learning plan*. This learning plan is rooted in the brand's business goals, and organized by the patient and professional journeys. For each stage of the stakeholder journey (whether patient or professional), there are specific business objectives tied to a RM campaign. In turn, each business objective carries with it hypotheses for testing, and specific metrics for confirming or altering those hypotheses. The metrics may come from consumer market research, secondary Rx audit data, or behavioral transactions (such as calls, registrations, or online activity).

SUBJECT	OBJECTIVE (What We Want to Learn)	METRICS FOR SUCCESS (What We Will Learn)	DATA & MEASUREMENT TOOLS (How We Will Learn)	MARKETING DECISIONS AND IMPLICATIONS (How We Will Use The Learning)
Acquisition	■ Test and identify the most cost-effective means of acquiring qualified leads	■ Response rates to promotion by source ■ Engagement, content consumption, registration ■ Breakouts by promotional source	■ Registration database, ■ Website analytics	■ Optimize acquisition media and tactics
Conversion	■ Determine how effective various initiatives are at driving conversion	■ Incremental product usage (Rx) for RM participants	■ Anonymous Patient-level Rx, claims ■ Self-reported product usage	■ Optimize product and patient support materials. ■ Examine cost structure
Adherence	■ Test and identify the most cost-effective means of enrolling patients and caregivers into the program ■ Determine how effective the program is at driving compliance and persistence	■ Increase in product persistence and compliance	■ Anonymous Patient-level Rx, claims ■ Self-reported product usage	■ Optimize registration vehicles ■ Improve adherence tools
Advocacy	■ Patients sharing their positive product experiences with others	■ Submission of stories ■ Social media posts	■ Social media tracking tools ■ Tracking of online advocacy vehicles	■ Encourage patient dialogue

Figure 5.1   Learning plan framework

The format of the learning plan is illustrated in Figure 5.1. There is a row in each table corresponding to the phase of the consumer or professional journey that our fielded RM programs are intended to affect. For consumer programs, these phases are acquisition, conversion, adherence, and advocacy. For each phase, there are several components:

1. The *business objective* of each phase. This may be thought of alternately as: what is the RM program is trying to accomplish? What hypotheses are we testing? What do we want to learn?

2. The *specific metrics* to be consulted and tracked over time as a measure of success for thatphase. Another often used phrase for these success metrics is *key performance indicators,* or KPIs. Note that KPIs may be direct measurements or they may be calculated fields, and not every metric is a KPI, only those integral to evaluating one or more business goals.

    For example, a business goal for an acquisition campaign may be registering members in the RM program for further dialogue about a product. A natural KPI for this goal is the rate of growth of registrants in the CRM database. However, page views of the website registration page is not by itself a KPI, but merely an intermediate measurement in the funnel, toward the larger goal.

    Another important point should be made about KPIs: they may be measured for the overall RM program population, or they may be broken out by segment. Segmentations can take many forms: by source of leads, geography, demographics, stakeholder attitudes or behaviors. The best segmentations to use are ultimately rooted in the campaign strategy, as described in the previous chapter.

3. The *data and measurement tools* that will be employed to make the measurements, these may be a combination of primary research or secondary data. The secondary data may be directly measured patient or professional behavior showing interactions with the RM program. Alternatively, it may be ancillary demographic, psychographic, or corporate data that is used as background context, or the basis for segmentation. It is useful to write these information sources down explicitly as part of the learning plan, in case data needs to be purchased, or retrieved from a database within another department.

4. *Implications and marketing decisions* that will be made as a result of significant levels or trends in these measurements. Writing these down explicitly insures that analysis is not taking place in a vacuum, but rather is integral to the decision-making process. Marketing

decisions may be made from a single measurement, or as a result of multiple, confluent findings from KPIs that reinforce the same conclusion.

For example, within the acquisition phase of CRM program, if a particular media channel (a website banner placement, or a print ad) is unusually expensive with a high response rate, so that the cost per qualified lead (CPQL) is much higher than other tactics, the marketing decision may be to remove that media tactic from the next campaign.

The learning plan is most effective when the pharmaceutical manufacturer client, and all related agencies and vendors, develop the plan collaboratively, at the beginning of the project, and before the RM program goes live in market. All parties should agree to this measurement blueprint and should share the success metrics within each of their companies

Let's go across each row of Figure 5.1 and spell out the primary elements of the learning plan for a CRM program:

- *Acquisition*: a primary business objective is to encourage consumers or professionals to go beyond just awareness, and to learn in depth about the product, and ultimately register and give permission (also called "opting-in") to receive additional communications. Indeed, from an RM perspective, acquisition literally means the contact information is "acquired" into the database. The degree of product learning is measured by *engagement,* meaning the viewing by consumers of multiple product-related content areas. We shall provide examples of engagement tracking within a later chapter. The acquisition is measured by registration in the RM database.

These measures are all calculated by the segment of promotional source. Say there are multiple acquisition media channels driving to a common product website, as illustrated in Figure 5.2. Engagement of product-related content on the website should be tracked for each media source, whether print, online, Direct response television advertising (DRTV), in-office, or direct marketing. Particular weighting should be given to goal-oriented activities like CRM registration, patient screening questionnaires, and discussion guides for patients when they visit their physician. Another acquisition-related KPI example is CPQL, which is derived from the count of unique database leads,

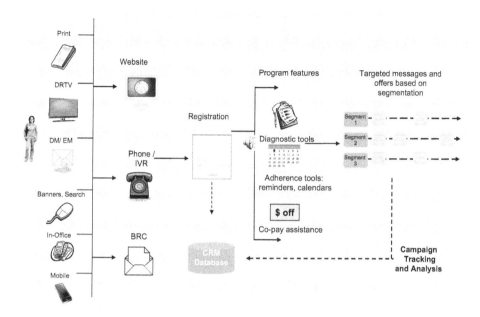

Figure 5.2   Consumer relationship marketing and the learning plan

who are qualified based on contact information and survey answers, divided into the cost of an acquisition medium. As to be discussed in the measurement chapter (Chapter 7), this enables marketing decisions to be optimized toward the most efficient promotional channels.

Conversion: for CRM, the business objective for conversion is to evaluate how the program is contributing to incremental filling of patient prescriptions. The KPIs to evaluate this can come from either primary research (self-reported prescription usage from CRM users versus a control group), or secondary data (product prescriptions of CRM participants versus a control group, measured through anonymized patient-level claims). For either of these, breaking out by segment is quite informative, either the segment of the acquisition promotional source, or other segmentation based on demographic, behavioral, or attitudinal attributes reported from questionnaires.

- *Adherence*: the business questions to be answered are related to both registering patients into an adherence program, as well as the actual improvement of patient adherence to the medication regimen. Registration is mostly about optimizing the alternative sign-up mechanisms, whether they come within starter kits, websites, or in response to a CRM communication. As for increased adherence by

CRM patients, the components of compliance (taking medication as directed) and persistence (staying on medication long term) should be evaluated separately, and by segment where possible. These can be measured with anonymized patient-level claims data, as well as self-reported questionnaire results.

- *Advocacy*: consumer advocacy programs are not extensively developed in pharmaceutical markets, due to regulations around incentives and reporting of adverse events. However, they are more prevalent in other health and wellness categories like nutrition, cosmetics, and fitness. Advocacy can take place in either a structured on unstructured way. The structured methods include asking consumers or patients to share their product experience with the manufacturer, or to recommend to a friend. Materials encouraging this, paper-based or digital, can be coded and tracked for spreading a "viral marketing" promotion. Unstructured advocacy takes place within social media channels, as consumers blog, text, or tweet their experiences and recommendations to their friends and followers without moderation. This activity can be measured with social media scraping and measurement software, and follow-on analyses on trends and conversation topics.

For PRM, there are many similarities yet notable differences in the learning plan.

- Acquisition is still related to cost-effectively gathering leads into a database, and so measurement of CPQL by promotional source is still a valid KPI. The same holds for engagement within program touch points. The marketing decisions related to optimizing budgets toward more efficient tactics with high response and engagement rates also apply to PRM.

- Trial is the term used within PRM as the next stage, signifying that physicians are showing initial prescribing of the product. Physician-level prescription data can be used or account-level purchase data.

- The next phase of PRM is adoption and signifies increased and regular product prescribing. Similar metrics are used as in the adoption phase, yet an increase in market share is expected. In addition, adoption can also mean participation of healthcare professionals (HCPs) in the value-added services that the manufacturer is providing, as well as acknowledgement in primary research that the professionals think of the manufacturer as a value provider beyond products.

- Advocacy within PRM relates to physicians sharing their positive experiences prescribing products and seeing results in their patients. It can also mean professionals informing colleagues about the services provided within PRM programs. Measurement of advocacy is still in its infancy, but signs can be detected within online physician communities, as well as traditional activity at medical conventions, speaker programs, and in medical journals, printed or online.

Selecting the Best Information Sources for Measurement

Within the learning plan development, it is critical to identify the right information sources for measurement and tracking. The pharmaceutical data landscape is a dynamic one and to gain an updated perspective we have turned to multiple industry information experts for their advice. While specific identities of these experts cannot be disclosed, the discussion is summarized below:

Haimowitz: How critical is it for pharmaceutical companies to measure the impact of CRM programs?

Information Experts: Certainly adherence is a very critical marketing initiative, and CRM programs have almost always shown a positive return on persistence and compliance. One example is the "product plus," where patients are given, with their medication, resources to answer questions and track progress, including call center and online support.

Haimowitz: What data sources have proven valuable in better marketing to consumers?

Information Experts: Anonymized patient-level, longitudinal data enables us to really measure if there has been an impact; specifically, did the patients within an adherence the CRM program fill one more script? IMS and SDI are the leading vendors here, and they have been increasing in completeness. In the best case, almost three-quarters of the prescriptions in their retail panel have some longitudinal patient component. There are fewer problems than in past years with patients dropping off due to switching insurers or switching stores. This is due to employment of proprietary hashing algorithms that are used across multiple pharmacy stores within the retail panels; different stores will use these hashing algorithms to compute the same anonymous pseudo-customer number across stores, which allows for continuity of patient longitudinal prescription tracking.

Haimowitz: Can these patient-level longitudinal data sources be mapped to physicians as well?

Information Experts: Yes, increasingly so, to provide patterns that enable us to have insight as to compare physicians on how compliant or persistent their patients are. This in principle can identify which physicians are the prime targets for adherence programs. Whereas patient compliance programs run through vendors like Catalina or Adheris can be impactful on patient share, this will enable the overlay of the sales channel. That may enable the sales force, or non-personal promotion (NPP), to inform certain physicians that patient adherence is an issue in their practice. However, regulatory issues still exist before this can become a reality.

Haimowitz: What other data sources have proven valuable in better marketing to consumers?

Information Experts: We have also been making increased use of third-party consumer data sources like Experian to understand the demographic and psychographic makeup of consumers, both in general, and specific to our CRM programs.

Haimowitz: What data sources have proven valuable in better marketing to HCPs?

Information Experts: Group practices affiliation information is growing in importance, and it is beneficial to standardize around a leading, consistent source to insure quality. This enables us to take "account management" selling more seriously, results can be measured across components of a group. This enables us to assess how much homogeneity of prescribing there may be within a group practice. Another example, with the onset of tablet-based selling, is the data stream of slide presentations made by the sales representatives to the HCPs. This information from the tablets is becoming really critical in guiding messaging strategies. It will become even more so with some states limiting prescriber-level data (as true in Vermont and New Hampshire in early 2010)

The leading data vendors have also begun storing some of the insurance copay information as part of the retail panel data. This opens up the opportunity to have a dialogue with physicians that "X percent of your patients are paying no more than $Y for this medication."

Haimowitz: How successful has the pharmaceutical industry been in coordinating "personal" and "non-personal" promotion to HCPs?

Information Experts: There has been limited success with particular brands. Until recently, personal and NPPs were exclusive, and the sales management were concerned about non-personal. Now, with many large pharmaceutical companies reducing their sales forces, and with more "no-see" physicians and practices, there is decreased call frequency. Now, pharma companies are looking for the synergies between these channels. The non-personal channels used most often are outbound-generated direct mail and phone. Companies are also increasing use of video detailing services. However, it is not cheap, and targeting is required to restrict who can have access to a video detail. The cost is roughly the same to a pharmaceutical company as a personal sales call. It is difficult to make money on this when implemented for just one product at a time; a portfolio approach is more sensible.

Haimowitz: Why is it important to a pharmaceutical company to have a "360-degree view" on HCPs?

Information Experts: Certainly from a positive aspect, it is helpful for better understanding the interests of HCPs, and to offer them enhanced services. It would also be great to inform the personal sales force of the other ways their called-on physicians are interacting with the company, so we have a continuous dialogue from digital to sales reps. In addition, this 360-degree view may enable companies to control costs; pharmaceutical firms want to optimize promotion, and to avoid wasting resources.

There is a defensive reason as well. The more reliant companies become on non-personal promotion, the greater the threat is that HCPs may be bombarded with too many frequent contacts from different sources, causing an HCP to be alienated from a manufacturer. Coordination of contacts is critical. In principle, we should be asking professionals, "How do you wish to be communicated with?" and focus dialogue within that preferred channel. As of now, however, the implemention of this is more theory than fact.

In-Market Testing and Experimental Design

As mentioned in our development of the learning plan above, many of the business objectives are to test which among a set of alternatives is the best option for that program. Usually, RM creative and messages are tested in primary research to determine whether they resonate with a focus group of the target segment of consumers or HCPs.

In the case that, after the research has taken place, multiple options are still viable, then in-market testing should be a component of your learning plan. As an example, consider testing a banner advertisement that is geared to driving response and registration as part of an acquisition campaign for a CRM program. There may be (at least) four different dimensions of the banner that can vary:

1. The creative on the banner, for which three options are developed:

    •   patient image, solid background, or nature scene.

2. The call to action, which has two text options:

    •   "sign up for information" or "sign up for up to $30 off your first prescription."

3. The size of the banner, large or small.

4. The placement, top of page, versus side of page.

Therefore, in all there are $3 \times 2 \times 2 \times 2 = 24$ different banner options.

The product consumer marketing team running the CRM program wants to understand which banner has the most impact. In addition, the marketing team wants to understand what the key factors were that determined the success of the banner.

This is an example of a marketing tactics requiring an *experiemental design*. In order to complete this design, first, the metric for evaluating competing banners must be chosen to determine the winner. Let's say this choice is the *click through rate,* or the percentage of banner exposures resulting in a click toward the website.

Next the choice must be made as to the count and the actual design of which banners will be put into market. Three, often used, experiemental options in direct marketing are illustrated below:

A/B TEST DESIGN

In an A/B test design, a small number of options (typically two) are both placed in market, and that with the highest response rate is the winner. In the case of the CRM acquisition campaign, three banners may be chosen that differ by only one dimension:

- solid background, information call to action, large, top of page;

- patient image, information call to action, large, top of page;

- nature scene, information call to action, large, top of page.

After some time in market, click through rates are measured, and the banner with the higher ratio (say the nature scene) is selected as the winner. Furthermore, it can be learned that the nature scene was the most responsive creative.

Even less informative would have been an A/B test design where two unrelated banners were chosen based on the marketers' hunch:

- nature scene, information call to action, large, top of page;

- patient image, discount call to action, large, side of page.

In this case, a winner can still be chosen based on click through rate, but it would not be apparent at all what factors drove that better response.

The benefits of the A/B test design is that it is easy to implement and determine a winner, and at times the results lead to conclusions about the drivers of response. The drawback is that only some of the options are considered, and nothing is learned about some of the dimensions (in this case, call to action, size, or placement). In other words, a local optimum may have been chosen, but there is no guarantee of a global optimum.

Full Factorial Test Design

In a full factorial test design, all combinations of marketing tactics are fielded, and randomly presented as impressions with equal weight. In the case of the CRM acquisition banner advertisements above, that means 24 banners would be placed on a given media placement, and response rates would be gathered for each. An analysis would then determine exactly which combination of the four factors had the highest click through rate of response.

FRACTIONAL FACTORIAL TEST DESIGN

There are times when a full factorial design is not attainable, due to a low expected in-market total impression volume, which will mean not enough statistical power to perform a thorough analysis. In these cases, a *fractional factorial* design can be used. A fractional factorial test design places a reduced number of options in market, (roughly half is often used) but wisely constructs them so that learnings can still be made regarding which of the primary effects are contributing to the high response rate.

See Dean and Voss (1998) as one of many textbooks that provide a more thorough treatment of design of experiments, with related statistical models and tables.

MATCHED MARKETS LOCAL TEST PILOT

In the beginnings of a company's RM capabilities, when budgets may be modest, there may not be enough support to roll out a program across the entire country. In this case, one way to proceed is with a pilot in one or more geographic test markets, typically metropolitan areas corresponding to media selection (such as designated market areas (DMAs)). Then, control markets are chosen to match each test market, based on similarity on as many of these conditions as follows:

- geographic location;

- relevant product market shares;

- managed care environment;

- sales force coverage;

- similar consumer population demographics.

Thus, Miami and Tampa-St. Petersburg (two Florida cities) may potentially serve as matched markets in a CRM pilot. However, Miami and Boston are unlikely to because of different geographies, different demographics, and differing insurance coverage mix.

Once the local test markets and corresponding control cities are chosen, the CRM or PRM program is fielded within the test markets only. Then, over time, measurements for awareness, conversion, and adherence are statistically compared in a basic hypothesis test (such as a statistical T-test) between the test market areas and their corresponding control markets.

Pro-Forma Analysis of Relationship Marketing Impact

As part of the strategic design of a RM program, one should do a basic analysis to determine financial feasibility of the program. This is typically called a *pro forma analysis*, which is an estimated calculation of costs and revenues associated with a program, in order to justify the expenses. In this section we will illustrate the basic approach to a pro-forma analysis.

The most basic stage of this is a breakeven analysis, in which it is determined what level of incremental conversion and adherence is required to cover costs. For example, to use rough numbers, say an upcoming CRM program has an estimated media cost of $3,000,000 and an estimated total fees for agencies, vendors, and production of $2,000,000.

Presume that the primary objective of the program is to convert new patients to therapy, with no expected lift in adherence within the first campaign. Say that the estimated lifetime value to the pharmaceutical company of a new patient on therapy is $500.

Then, in order to meet the expected costs of the program, the number of incremental patients converted to therapy is:

($3,000,000 + $2,000,000) / $500 = 10,000 incremental conversions to product

Now, say that the incremental conversion rate of CRM database registrants is 25 percent higher than a matched control group of other consumers with the same demographics and medication history.

Then, the number of CRM database registrants required to break even is:

10,000 / 25% = 40,000

In order to have revenue equal to twice the investment, then the number of CRM database registrants required is 80,000.

Now, with 80,000 registrants, the estimated incremental sales from conversion alone is $10,000,000. What if there was also an adherence gain? Say 15 percent of the registrants also joined the adherence program, and that the adherence program raised the lifetime value 20 percent, or an additional $100. Then the additional adherence gain is:

$100 * (15% * 80,000) = $1,200,000

In a later chapter on Measurement (Chapter 7) we shall discuss the calculation of *return on investment (ROI)* as:

(incremental sales – cost) / cost

For this hypothetical campaign the ROI is:

($11.2 MM – $5.0 MM) / $5.0 MM = 1.24

This essentially spells out the approach to a pro-forma model: a rough estimation of costs, to demonstrate potential profitability of this model. In this case, with the adherence impact also added, we know that at 40,000 registrants we are just above breakeven (ROI of 0.12), and at 80,000 registrants there is an ROI of 1.24.

A natural question that follows is: how many responders can be expected with the stated media investment? This requires an understanding of direct marketing response rates and timing of the response curves.

Promotion Response Rates and Curves

Each acquisition tactic that drives consumers to respond will yield a distinct volume of CRM registrants, and at a different pace of time. We call a response curve of an acquisition tactic the functional form of responders over time for that tactic. Response curves generally appear as in Figure 5.3. The X axis in the figure represents the time since that promotional piece is in market, starting at the first date in market (at zero), and may continue for up to several months or even years. In RM, typically performance data is gathered and tracked weekly, and thus the timescale of data points are usually one week apart. The Y axis represents the number of responders to that direct response piece within a particular time interval.

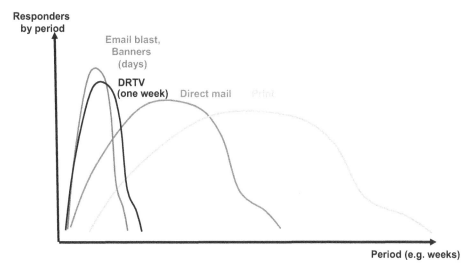

Figure 5.3   **Promotion response curves for consumer relationship marketing registration**

The general pattern of the response curve is the same sequence regardless of the promotional tactic, consisting of four stages:

1.   *Initiation*: the time period where responses begin.

2.   *Acceleration*: the period with increasing responses week by week.

3.   *Plateau*: a period where weekly responses remain constant, and begin to decrease.

4.   *Descent*: a period where weekly responses decrease toward zero.

Different promotional tactics can show marked variations within this response curve framework. As shown in Figure 5.3, each channel has an inherent scale of the response timings. Internet tactics such as banner impressions and search engine results tend to yield a response within one to two days; the same can be said for direct email campaigns. Direct mail yields responses over two to six weeks after the mail is dropped. Print advertisements with business reply cards show a peak response over two to three months after the issue date, but the descent phase can last for as long as two years.

Estimated Response Rates By Channel

As for the rates of response, there are published direct response rates by industry available each year from the Direct Marketing Association (DMA 2009) and statistics cited in RM textbooks like Stone and Jacobs (2008, Chapter 21). Note that response rates have been dramatically decreasing in multiple media. Direct mail response rates have dropped during the past few decades from a range of 3 to 4 percent down to a range of 1 to 2 percent. For example, from a direct mail drop to 100,000, a total of 1,000 to 2,000 database registrants may be expected. Of course, the ultimate response rate depends upon the quality of the target list, and how compelling the creative and offer are.

Printed business reply cards (BRCs) within consumer publications can yield a highly variable response, depending on the publication, but as a ratio of overall circulation may vary from tenths of one percent to small percentage numbers. Typically the BRCs are an effective response tool within print, and may work in synergy with websites and toll-free numbers as a response mechanism. Direct response calls to action within television advertisements are also quite variable; drive to toll-free numbers and websites are most effective from TV. Print and television also have the additional branding effects that make them attractive, despite the high costs.

An electronic mail (email) response rate is made up of two components:

1.   *email open rate*, the percentages of emails received that are opened; and

2.   *email click through rate*, the percentage of opened emails that are clicked on a link driving to the target website for registration.

Email industry sources can give benchmarks, and the reader should realize that in the days of crowded inboxes and Spam, open rates are decreasing. The quality of the list plays a critical role. High-quality lists for healthcare may have an open rate approaching 10 to 20 percent, and a compelling message with a clear call to action can yield an email click through rate of 15 to 25 percent.

For banner advertisements, click through rates to websites are usually in the neighborhood of 0.01 to 0.1 percent as a fraction of impressions (which are in the millions), and that must be multiplied with the website registration rate (often single digit percentages) to get overall acquisition response rates. Search engine click through rates are highly dependent on the quality of search phrases, but are usually an order of magnitude higher than banner ads.

HCP response rates to register at PRM website portals are not as well understood, due to the novelty of PRM promotion. Generally, the expectation is for response rates to be higher than those for consumer campaigns, since the calls to action are professionally oriented and more likely to be relevant. One may also consult the business to business response rates of a source like the DMA response rate handbook (DMA 2009).

Forecasting Responders to Consumer Relationship Marketing Acquisition Tactics

With a media plan in place, and with estimated response rates timings per media tactic, one can develop a rough estimate of registration levels stemming from a planned CRM acquisition campaign. Table 5.1 overleaf illustrates this approach:

Table 5.1 demonstrates a summary level worksheet of how a forecast can be made for CRM registrants. For each media category on the left, fill in the universe of exposures, whether they are impressions, circulation, or volume of the direct communication. It is also important to add the scheduled timing of the media tactics. Then, using low and high estimates of response rates by category, one completes a range of registrants into the CRM database.

However, that number of registrations is not the most meaningful for planning the CRM campaign. The next few columns make the estimates more realistic. First, there is a discount percentage to what percentage of the registrants are qualified, meaning they leave contact information and are in the

Table 5.1   Forecasting estimated responders to a CRM campaign

Media Category	Impressions/ Circulation	Placement (month, year)	Registrations (low, high)	Qualified percent	Overlap percent	Unique qualified reg. (low, high)
Direct mail						
Email						
Banners						
Search						
Print						
TOTALS						

target segment of the campaign (for example, within the correct age range, or at a certain stage of the patient journey). This percentage is usually more than half, because mostly those consumers for whom the offer is valuable are those that will register. However, this percentage can vary by media tactic. The next column signifies an overlap percentage, because there may be consumers that register from multiple sources. This percentage is typically quite low, less than 10 percent, but should be accounted for to avoid duplication.

Finally, the last column signifies the unique qualified lead estimates for that media category. This range is calculated by taking the registration range, and then multiplying across first by the qualified rate, and then (1- overlap rate).

There are several enhancements to this table, where the next level of detail can be provided along any of these dimensions:

- *Media tactics*: the rows of Table 5.1 can be expanded to itemize by specific media tactics, such as individual publications, direct mail list, website properties, or search engines. This will give more specificity on the forecasts.

- *Timing of responses*: in addition to total responses, the timing by week or month of the registrants can be broken down based on prototypical response curves, as we discussed earlier. For example, a direct mail drop to 100,000 consumer targets in early May can be modeled as having a total registrants of 1,000 to 2,000, with 45 percent in May, 45 percent in June, and 10 percent in July.

- *Cost:* one can include the fully-loaded costs for each media tactic (including media placement, materials development, production and postage as applicable). That enables one to calculate for each media tactic the CPQL, which in turn enables optimization of media planning based on the expected registration rates.

In a later chapter, we shall illustrate measurement dashboards and reports that track actual in-market RM campaign results, and compare to a forecast based on history and on the media plan. The comparison of recent findings to the forecast can be what determines insight for future decision making and optimization.

Operations Resource Planning Based on Forecasts

The forecasted response and registration rates described in the previous section can be utilized for operational planning of a CRM campaign. Whether the forecast is weekly or monthly, this can help with planning different resources:

- *Call center staffing*: call centers that respond to a CRM acquisition campaign may be handled completely by interactive voice response (IVR), or they may be partly or completely staffed by "live agent" personnel who are trained to answer product or CRM program questions. With a forecast of responders by week, this can assist in staff planning. Note that not every caller will actually be a registrant. If one estimates that roughly half the people calling will register, then one should *double* the registrants column of Table 5.1 to get the number of responders. Remember, one also must take into account the percentage of responders that will be by phone, versus website.

- *Fulfillment:* printed materials, such as welcome kits, diagnostic screening tools, educational brochures, or adherence trackers are often mailed directly to registrants of a CRM or PRM program. The forecast of unique qualified registrants from Table 5.1 can be used to forecast a range of how many fulfillment packages are required to print, and what staffing is required at a fulfillment center to distribute. Of course, if fulfillment is primarily done electronically, via emails and PDF documents, then the costs and personnel associated with fulfillment are not as big a concern.

Continuing Case Study with ABC Pharmaceuticals and ABCOS

We will continue with our case study of our fictitious ABC Pharmaceuticals and their pre-launch planning of the osteoporosis once-monthly medication called ABCOS. As a setup, we will provide a media plan that is developed for a CRM program for ABCOS, and ask follow-up questions.

The ABCOS brand marketing team has planned the following targeted promotional media plan for several months after launch, during the first half of 2012. The tactics are itemized below:

$1.5 million in print direct response media advertising with BRCs:

- Women's Shelter magazines at $250,000 each:

    - February and April issues of Better Homes and Gardens

    - March and May issues of Southern Living.

- Health Magazines at $150,000 each:

    - February issue of Prevention

    - March issue of Self.

- Mature magazines at $200,000 each:

    - May issue of AARP.

$4 million in direct response television:

- $2 million on Lifetime during April and May

- $2 million on Oxygen during April and May.

$3 million in online advertising:

- $1.5 million in paid search campaigns on Google, Yahoo, and Bing from February to June:

    - $100,000 for each month from February to June.

    - Clicks drive to home page of www.ABCOS.com with search campaign code retained.

$1.5MM in paid banner advertising on WebMD, Yahoo Health, and Revolution Health during February to June:

- Clicks drive to home page of www.ABCOS.com with banner code retained.

The ABCOS team also has decided to test a direct mail campaign, licensing a list of 100,000 names of menopausal women who have said they suffering from osteoporosis. Members of this list will be mailed a small brochure on ABCOS that also encourages ABCOS CRM registration. Postage costs for the direct mail is 50 cents per piece.

There will be a fixed cost of $1 million to build the RM database for ABCOS and develop the associated reporting. ABC Pharmaceuticals is leveraging the CRM infrastructure of its other products. The ABCOS team is paying their agencies and media buyers a total of $3.5 million this year on creative development, production, and fulfillment.

On each direct response advertisement will be a consistent visual creative and consistent message emphasizing the new mechanism of action and also stressing showing the strong efficacy rates versus placebo. A secondary point is the minimal safety risks. The advertisements will offer to those who register:

- a free lifestyle magazine;

- a brochure about the changes of menopause;

- literature about ABCOS; and

- an ABCOS branded screener and checklist for patients to take to their physician.

Responders can specify whether they want to receive these items by email PDFs, or printed materials by postal mail. All advertising tactics will have a distinct toll-free phone number such as 1-877-ABC-2345, and a specific website URL such as self.ABCOS.com. The print magazines advertisements will all have BRCs with codes at the bottom specific to that magazine issue. All response mechanisms will be coded appropriately to insure that registrants can be tracked to specific media sources

The ABCOS brand team hopes that by Q2 and Q3 2012 they will be able to measure if this CRM campaign has helped achieve its objectives of:

1.   raising awareness of ABCOS;

2.   getting responses of patients into its CRM database;

3.   increasing new patient starts on ABCOS.

Concurrently, the ABCOS sales force will be targeting the 10,000 leading prescribers within the osteoporosis category using presentations on sales tablets, and will be encouraging physicians to visit and register on the professional section of ABCOS.com to learn more about the product. ABC Pharmaceuticals is also investing in a series of three Epocrates Doc-alerts via mobile devices shortly after product launch, as well as video details on HCP website portals that describe ABCOS to those physicians searching for information on menopause or osteoporosis.

Exercises for Chapter 5

Exercise 5.1 How are the consumer objectives for ABCOS being met by the media mix? Comment on the relative mix of digital versus print media, and whether this is appropriate for the disease category and the consumer demographic.

Exercise 5.2 What are the business objectives for PRM and how well are the tactical suggestions meeting those?

Exercise 5.3 Develop a learning plan for the ABCOS CRM program.

Exercise 5.4 Develop a learning plan for the ABCOS PRM program.

Exercise 5.5 Given the promotional planning for ABCOS CRM that was spelled out at the end of this chapter, what is a range of response rates that might be expected for each tactic? What is the range of the grand total of CRM registrations responses that we might expect?

6

Execution: Placing in the Marketplace

Thus far in this book we have discussed developing strategies for healthcare relationship marketing (RM) programs, rooted in fundamentals like the product lifecycle and the patient and professional journeys. This chapter is about how the strategy is realized with an execution of specific communication channels and marketing tactics.

We begin this chapter with a discussion of the movement of healthcare RM to digital, and why this is happening. We will discuss the benefits and caveats of digital RM.

Then we will turn our attention to selecting particular tactical decisions when executing each phase of the RM campaign: acquisition, conversion, and adherence (or loyalty for primary care physician (PCPs)). We will discuss how to determine the best promotional channels and how to establish the timings of touch points and dialogue with members of a consumer relationship marketing (CRM) or professional relationship marketing (PRM) program.

This chapter includes a detailed discussion on setting up the operational readiness for a RM campaign. We will outline steps on how to insure reliable and measurable data transmission by source. Also to be covered are the business rules and related software for distributing communications, and for updating the RM database.

Finally, we discuss operational monitoring and troubleshooting of a healthcare RM campaign; how to detect if there is an anomaly, and what course corrections to take.

The Movement Toward Digital Relationship Marketing

In ever increasing proportions, CRM is being conducted over the Internet. We will use interchangeably terms like "Internet-based," "digital," and "online." RM on the Internet provides a number of advantages over traditional offline tactics based on print or phone:

- *Cost efficiencies*: the economies of scale for digital are remarkable when compared to traditional offline channels. For example, the incremental cost of emailing an extra 10,000 members in a database is miniscule, compared to what that cost would be for direct mail.

- *Behavioral targeting*: digital media tactics, such as display banners and search terms, can be placed on web properties based on a visitor's behavior on related websites. The online media can also be focused to particular pages related to a specific therapeutic category. Online media buys can also be structured as "cost per acquisition," minimizing the risk in a campaign really aimed at acquiring members into an RM database.

- *Speed of data collection*: data is collected and available very rapidly after marketing tactics are deployed. As a result, Internet findings can be interpreted quite quickly, and can serve as a leading indicator of performance of other offline marketing tactics, and an early harbinger of prescription growth.

- *In-market testing*: due to the economies of scale and the high volumes of online visitors, in-market tests (as discussed in Chapter 5) can be implemented quickly and affordably. There is also software available from companies such as Omniture and Webtrends which enable straightforward implementation of these online tests and comparison of click through rates among alternatives.

Unfortunately, not all aspects of digital marketing are positive and it does have its disadvantages:

- *Limited response rate*: while impressions of banner advertisements and search engine tiles may be huge, the response rates are not.

When searching for a popular health term like "diabetes" or "pain" the result is a wide, diffuse scattering of results, meaning it can be difficult or expensive to achieve a high ranking. Furthermore, as discussed in Chapter 5, click through rates below 1 percent are the norm.

- *Demographic bias:* for consumers in their teens and twenties, online channels, including Internet and mobile, are indispensible. This demographic is primarily a target for maintaining wellness. For patients in their 50s and 60s, on multiple chronic medications, the Internet and mobile have a limited, focused role, and are less pervasive.

- *Limited guidelines by regulators:* at the time of writing, the US Food and Drug Administration (FDA) had not yet definitively ruled on guidelines for pharmaceutical promotion within social media, and there were still evolving practices in pharmaceutical paid search marketing. The lack of accepted practices can cause some manufacturers to be tentative in this channel.

A recent 2010 research report compiled by L2 (Luxury Lab) and PhD Media (L2 2010) provides some perspective on the role of digital marketing: The study noted that, as a portion of pharmaceutical direct to consumer (DTC) advertising spend, the digital channel had increased 31 percent year over year, yet still remains at only 4 percent of DTC spending. This study also ranked 51 consumer pharmaceutical brands based on their digital aptitude. Not surprisingly, the highest scoring brands in the report where aimed at youth (18–30) markets, most notably female contraceptives. Indeed, in order to market to that demographic, a company must deliver via mobile, social, and web. Many of the highest ranked consumer pharmaceutical brands also had years left on their product lifecycle. Conversely, as expected, cardiovascular drugs were generally ranked in the lower scoring category. For cardiovascular products, the target demographic age range is consumers in their 50s and 60s. Furthermore, many hypertension and cholesterol-lowering medications have gone generic or are nearing their loss of exclusivity.

So, in considering consumer awareness and acquisition media, consider your target. Do research into the channels and media that really target your consumer. For some therapeutic categories, don't give up on focused print, or focused demographically matched direct response television advertising

(DRTV), or even targeted direct mail or email lists. Digital is one important arrow in your quiver, but not the whole arsenal. Your digital investment and innovation should align to your brand's needs and your target.

Selecting Consumer Relationship Marketing Touch Points Based on Personas and Experiences

In Chapter 4 we described the development of personas that illustrate representative members of target segments of our RM programs, and we also discussed experience maps that exemplify what media are consumed and what communication channels are employed by these persona. The experience maps also highlight the decisions that our personas make as they move along the intended patient or professional journeys.

These experience maps are in fact a blue print for selection of the touch points within the CRM or PRM program. They help the marketing brand team form a strategy in what components to include: precisely those elements that are critical to personas moving along the patient and professional journey.

At times, it may be innovative and tempting to implement the latest marketing solution. Starting in 2009, there has been a rise of healthcare companies creating a presence on social media properties like Facebook or YouTube. As of 2010, most of these executions were rooted in corporate communications. At the time of writing this book, the first pharmaceutical brands have been experimenting with Facebook pages, or YouTube video channels. The social media presences can be made to appear and behave like the home page of a branded website. Yet these alone do not form a strategy, and they must not be disconnected from the overall target's experience.

Consider the category of cosmetic pharmaceuticals, like dermal fillers, that aim to help make people appear years younger, as with a facelift. A Facebook page in this category can contain extensive product information, a doctor finder, and before and after pictures. It must also include fair balance as well. The sections can be divided as panels, with most hyperlinked to interior pages on the product website. In this way, Facebook can be made to emulate an alternative home page, or perhaps thought of as a "landing page."

However, the question arises, from where are people landing? That is, what is the beginning of the prospect's user experience that gets them to Facebook? Here are some potential examples:

- A 40-something Facebook user sees a friend's post and perhaps photos of a friend who describes getting a facelift, or using "dermal filler." This can prompt our prospect to search within Facebook, and call up the particular product page.

- An offline advertisement (print, TV, in office, out of home) says, "see us on Facebook," prompting a prospect to search there.

The same careful planning should precede the execution within any other social media channels, for they are not islands that stand alone. People need to get there to view it. Consider YouTube for videos. Merely placing a patient instructional video on YouTube will not get that video viewed, nor patients converted to that particular device or treatment regimen. It needs to be supplemented with other awareness and acquisition tactics driving patients to that video. Thus, even though social media is growing as an acquisition component, and the 30 to 50-year-old demographics have been using these increasingly, marketers are encouraged to not build another island, but to think through the experience to get them there.

Professional Relationship Marketing Touch Point Strategy

Similar recommendations hold for PRM. While there are now many isolated options for non-personal promotion (NPP) such as handheld alerts, or electronic details with call center support, it is critical to have a touch point plan based on a strategy rooted in segmentation and targeting. There also needs to be an understanding of how PRM can integrate with the field sales force.

For example, let's revisit the three-tiered segmentation of healthcare professionals (HCPs) for an upcoming new product launch that we introduced in Chapter 4, and illustrated in Figure 4.4. Once these HCP segments are established, the appropriate RM channel plan can be determined for each segment. Tier 3 professionals will receive a non-personal focus (conventions, publications, general product website) with a goal of creating product awareness and brand value. Tier 2 professionals will also get special invitations to closed loop RM, with digital and tele-channel support. The goal for Tier 2 is to create comfort in prescribing the new product. Tier 1 professionals will get all of the above promotion, plus sales force personal coverage, integrated with full RM.

Note also that, in addition, customized messages may be adopted for each of these segments:

- Tier 1 professionals are early adopters, including a higher degree of specialists and thought leaders. They can receive a message touting the innovative nature of the product (new mechanism of action, extended release, and/or delivery mechanism). Tier 1 professionals may also be receptive to messages on efficacy for difficult-to-treat patients.

- Tier 2 and Tier 3 professionals would receive the core product messages on efficacy and safety, including clinical trial results.

Touch Points at the Patient and Provider Crossroads

Some innovative in-market tactics are worthy of consideration as they fall within the critical juncture of the patient physician dialogue, and can therefore contribute to the journeys of both patient and provider. Two examples of these are:

- In-office *registration tablets*: for example, Phreesia is an electronic version of the standard patient registration form which enables embedding of screening questionnaires and creation of patient-doctor discussion guides.

- *Early experience program:* these are specific versions of the standard patient starter kits that usually launch conversion and adherence RM programs. Really, they are more geared to patient and physician trial of newly launched pharmaceutical products. In the early experience program, an example of which is Infomedics, patients receive a discount on new prescription medications, and are asked to fill out surveys about their health conditions and the medication both before and after treatment. Physicians receive feedback on the survey answers, and thus on the efficacy of the new treatment in their own practice.

Executing the Professional Relationship Marketing Feedback Loop

Staying on PRM, for some companies an integral part of the PRM persona experience maps is the *feedback loop* by which the healthcare company's headquarters and sales force learn of the interactions that professionals are having with the NPP channels. Implementing such a feedback loop requires enhancements to information technology, as well as policy decisions.

From a technology perspective, see Figure 6.1 for how the traditional sales force automation systems need to be expanded to accompany an integrated PRM system with a feedback loop. Pictured in grey is the traditional sales force channel, including the sales representatives selling with laptops or tablets, with information coming from a sales force automation system like Siebel or Dendrite, that leverages call-sample detail activities, prescription data, and professional demographics. Typically, segmentation and targeting information is extracted via direct query, or SAS software statistical processes, and sent to the sales force automation (SFA) system. Even within the sales force promotion,

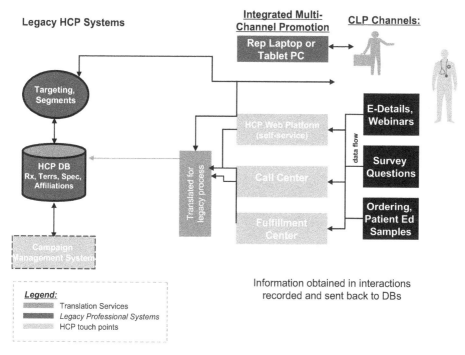

Figure 6.1   Infrastructure required for professional relationship marketing feedback loop

it is worth noting that the upgrade from paper-based visual aids to tablet-based selling results in a dramatic increase of data storage requirements, for tablets can now download a transactional history of all slides presented within a sales detail, for further analysis or feedback to the sales force or headquarters.

Aside from the sales force channel, data collection is now required at all non-personal touch points, illustrated in blue at the right of the figure. The call center, the PRM website, and the fulfillment center all have HCP-level data on transactions and survey results that could be leveraged. This information each needs to be filtered, summarized, translated into a common format (as pictured in green), and then stored in an expanded HCP database. With the expanded database, now decisions about future sales representative and NPP can be made based on a much wider set of information. For this reason, a more sophisticated campaign management system (pictured at lower left of Figure 6.2), must have business rules programmed that detect trends and changes in the distinct physician transaction types, and execute business rules for future targeting and messaging.

From a policy perspective, a healthcare manufacturer must make a decision on how to act upon certain information that may be discovered as part of this enhanced closed loop marketing (CLM) system. For example, if a physician visits a website portal outside of business hours and shows a strong interest in patient education, and this information is fed back to the sales force, how can a sales representative make use of this insight on the next call? Different companies may have distinct opinions on questions such as these:

- How much detail should representatives be given regarding the specific non-person contacts made by the HCPs they call on?

- Should representatives acknowledge whether they know that physician has visited the PRM website?

- Should representatives modify their detail based on the information received, such as emphasizing patient education in the next call? If so, how?

The decisions a company makes on these policies can affect data capture, processing, and storage requirements, as well as sales force training initiatives.

Design Principles of Websites for Relationship Marketing

In both consumer and professional relationship marketing, a branded website often serves as the hub of acquisition activity, as well as a source of detailed information, whether about a particular product or a portfolio of products. The website is usually the response destination for all digital acquisition media and mentioned within offline media as well. Given the critical nature of the website, it is worth mentioning these guidelines on website design especially for healthcare RM:

- develop landing pages for acquisition media that serve as a smooth transition from the promotional message, and that also encourage registration for RM;

- clearly depict intended website functionality and user experience flow as *wireframe* diagrams and associated specifications, and use those to reach team agreement on design and functionality;

- follow the standards of website usability, dating back to the work of Jakob Nielsen (Nielsen 1999) and more recently expressed in Nielsen and Tahir (2002).

- emphasize visitation to goal pages that move patients or professionals along the desired experience. This includes CRM or PRM registration most importantly. But there are other significant goal pages: in a recent study on digital pharmaceutical marketing (L2 2010, p. 14), there were revealing statistics on the frequency of certain features on branded product websites aimed at consumers. In particular:

    - 85 percent of branded websites have a doctor discussion guide available;

    - 57 percent of branded websites offer savings on first prescription on 57 percent of websites;

    - 42 percent offer savings for patients currently using a product;

    - 47 percent of branded websites are accompanied by an unbranded website, typically devoted to disease education.

- implement a clear funnel, or visitor pathways, that facilitate registration in RM programs.

Communication Contact Stream

A critical component of CRM programs is the stream of communications that members receive. The segmentation helps determine various components of communication:

- the channel (should be based on how the segment members communicate: whether it's direct mail, email, mobile, or social media);

- the timing (usually coincident with presumed healthcare decision points);

- the frequency (more valuable segments get more frequent communications).

We can think of a contact stream *CS* as a sequence of N communications that are segment dependent:

$$CS: S_i \longrightarrow <C_1(S_i, t_1), C_2(S_i, t_2), .., C_N(S_i, t_N)>$$

The communications occur at specific times based on the overall CRM program as well as the specific segment. For example, consider a CRM program related to children's nutrition, toys, or medications. There are natural milestones in a baby's development that can trigger purchase: birth, first solid foods, first words, first steps, and so on. A CRM design will trigger targeted communications to members shortly before each of these milestones are reached.

In addition, the C_j may vary by channel according to segment. One example of this is delivering mobile text messages to teenagers who are continually on their cell phones, and using email to communicate with older demographics. Often, channel is determined by explicit member preference. A CRM registration form can ask consumers whether they wish to receive future communications by postal mail versus email.

For PRM, there is also a need for communication contact streams, but these are less frequently tied to milestones of the professional and more to events related to the manufacturer company or to the product. Communications are sent out regarding new clinical research results, medical conventions, or a new product or service that the manufacturer is offering. Also relevant to PRM is asking about channel preference; professionals may wish to be updated by email, personal digital assistant (PDA) text message, direct mail, or even by in-office fax.

Consumer Relationship Marketing Database Development

The hub of all CRM activity is the centralized database, which stores all relevant information regarding registered consumers and their interactions with the RM program. A full description of a CRM database schema would be beyond the scope of this book. The reader is referred to Chapter 3 of Stone and Jacobs (2008) from a direct marketers approach, or for even more depth, see Todman (2000) from a data warehouse designers perspective.

The basic schematic of a RM database includes four types of tables:

1.   Customer data:

- contact information, including name, address, email, phone number (where appropriate);

- communication channel preferences;

- segmentation memberships;

- demographic data from third-party overlays.

2.   Transactional data for customers:

- registration histories, including opt-in status;

- inbound and outbound communications involving that customer;

- note that redemption of incentives, such as copay cards are linked to product usage, and are typically housed within a separate database of a Health Insurance Portability and Accountability Act (HIPAA)-compliant data partner.

3. Campaign information:

- question and answer pairs, for survey questions at registration or during ongoing dialogue;

- media flowcharts with spending;

- source code matrices (discussed later in this chapter);

- fulfillment codes and contents (also discussed later in this chapter).

4. Analytical data mart:

- summarized customer transaction histories for analysis;

- merged tables for use in modeling

The database is typically kept up to date upon some planned operational cycle, which may be daily, weekly, monthly, or some other variant. CRM databases in pharmaceuticals tend to fit a prescribed format, especially if designed by one of the leading healthcare database vendors. A partial list of these are Acxiom, Fair Isaac, Epsilon, Harte-Hanks, SAS, and Siebel. Other database suppliers also exist, and this is a dynamic marketplace.

Source Coding of Acquisition Media and Responses

One primary way of measuring and optimizing a CRM program is to optimize the acquisition media. We will get into the full calculation framework in the next chapter. However, pertinent to this chapter is the operational need to identify, for all registrants to the program, which in-market acquisition tactic led them to register.

OFFLINE MEDIA TRACKING

This tracking of registrants by acquisition source requires advanced operational planning well before the campaign is launched, indeed as all vendors are trained and in-market pieces are designed. Consider a CRM program, where registrants can sign up via website, phone, or business reply card (BRC). There may be dozens of acquisition tactics across digital channels, in-office materials, print, perhaps even DRTV and radio. Each of these tactics will have a registration call to action that includes one or more of:

- visit a website (specified by a URL);

- call a (toll-free) phone number;

- complete a printed registration

In order to track registrations by acquisition tactic, there need to be distinctions in the calls to action. This means:

- usage of distinct toll-free numbers per acquisition media;

- usage of alternate website "vanity" URLs that serve as aliases and pass through to a landing page on the website enabling registration;

- printed codes on the various registration forms that may be on BRCs, in-office brochures, or website PDF downloads.

Note that implementing all of these recommendations concurrently may be a challenge, as there are only so many memorable "vanity" phone numbers and website URLs that consumers will remember before taking action. However, marketers need to understand that the more specifically in-market tactics are coded, the more the sizable acquisition budget can be optimized.

In RM acquisition, there are various levels of detail at which tactics can be measured. In a typical consumer RM campaign, there are a wide range of acquisition channels via which consumers can register, and these are arranged in hierarchies. Consider print advertising. There are newspapers and magazines. Within magazines are categories like women's service, shelter, news, science, sports, and many others. Then within each category are specific magazines; for instance, the shelter category includes specific magazines like Better Homes and Gardens, Good Housekeeping, House Beautiful, and Southern Living. Finally, each magazine has multiple issues, monthly or quarterly.

The document that keeps a record of all registration sources for CRM leads is called the *source code matrix*. This document has a record, at a refined level, for every acquisition tactic that brings consumers into the CRM program. For example, for a springtime acquisition campaign in the women's health category, one record of the source code matrix might be the May 2010 *Good Housekeeping* magazine BRC. Another would be the second quarter 2010 Google paid search campaign.

Several dimensions can be found in the source code matrix for tracking and evaluation:

1. acquisition source name;

2. unique code for that source;

3. media channel:

    •   examples of media channel include in-office, print, online, mobile, and out of home;

4. tactic description, in free text;

5. in-market period, specified by a begin date and end date;

6. media category:

    •   usually this is a category of media, such as women's, health, news, shelter, and so on. There are also potential for subcategories that further specify each category, creating in effect a media hierarchy;

7. a unique code for that media source;

8. acquisition tactic costs:

    •   media spending;

- production costs;

9. circulation or impressions;

10. registration mechanisms (discussed above):

  - toll-free number;

  - website URL;

  - printed form code.

The source code matrix should be continually updated with each campaign or with each change.

ONLINE MEDIA TAGGING

For digital media promotion, there is a more specific process for source coding and for insuring that media responses are measurable as they generate leads to a website. That digital source coding process is called *tagging*. Tagging is essentially making additions to the source code of digital promotional files, whether they are banners, emails, or search campaigns tiles. The code snippets are typically generated from web analytics tracking software; examples of such software are Omniture, Webtrends, and Google Analytics. Once the digital promotional code is enhanced, then every in-market click of that promotion generates a tally to the web analytics software of the response, and further website engagement is tracked for that response.

Another type of tagging used to evaluate direct response media sources is called *spotlight tagging*. This enables digital media companies to determine when particular goal pages on the website are accessed by viewers of the online media tactic. Doubleclick is one leading supplier of spotlight tags: Atlas is another.

Finally, in order to measure digital media all the way through to registration, at times a media source parameter is passed within the URL as a visitor clicks through to the website. That parameter can be saved along with a completed registration form to ensure proper attribution of registrants to the source online media promotion.

Operations and Campaign Management for Pharmaceutical Relationship Marketing

The remainder of this chapter is devoted to operational processes that must be put into practice as part of the Execution phase for healthcare RM, either consumer or professional. Whether or not operations is one's particular specialty, it is valuable for each reader to become familiar with these processes. Because RM operations require coordination of multiple vendors and agencies, nearly all readers of this book will be exposed to some aspect of campaign operations, some more intimately than others.

CAMPAIGN BUSINESS RULES

The RM program intelligence and controls are typically encoded in a series of business rules, which dictate the flow of information to and from consumers. Business rules are of two primary types, outbound rules and inbound rules, depending on which way the communication flows, relative to the database. For those with computer science backgrounds, the format is similar to a finite state machine. One can also think of business rules as "IF, THEN" rules where the clauses within the "IF" part are known as antecedents, or preconditions, and the clauses within the "THEN" part are known as consequents, or postconditions. In the templates below, we will use the moniker of "consumer," but the structure applies equally well to HCPs that are members of a PRM program.

Outbound business rules take the following IF–THEN format:

IF consumer is a member of
    AND date is within <time period>
    AND previous communication <composition code> has been sent
THEN send communication <composition code>

An example of an outbound business rule related to registration is:

- If a consumer is a new registrant

- AND date is one day after the date of registration

- THEN send a welcome package via postal mail to the registrant's postal address

- THEN send an acknowledgement via email to the registrant.

Inbound business rules take the following IF–THEN format:

IF consumer is a member of <segments>
    AND date is within <time period>
    AND communication <composition code> has been received
    AND response is <response code>
THEN modify consumer segment to

An example of an inbound business rule related to a patient request might be:

- IF a consumer is an active member

- AND answers that she is taking branded medication X

- THEN modify customer segment to *Brand X user*

- THEN send a Brand X received email

    Note: this email can verify the communication was received, and include a hyperlink with more information about Brand X.

Even though our business rule definitions explicitly mention time ranges, these ranges may not be required. A business rule is called a *triggered event* if the preconditions within the "IF" part of the rule do not include a time range. Then, the post-condition actions in the "THEN" are wholly determined by consumer activities, and not the passage of time.

Note that *concurrency* of rules is an issue, as with any rules-based system. In other words, at any given time point, multiple business rules may apply to the same customer. For example, a time-based birthday greeting email may be scheduled at the same time a trigger-based newsletter email should be sent out due to a customer request. In such a case, both business rules would fire at the same time for the same customer, resulting in multiple communications sent concurrently to that customer. In order to better control concurrency, one should understand the campaign management system being used, and the abilities to set precedence relationships, or overrides.

A CRM system may consist of hundreds of business rules. They are typically organized by categories related to particular business objectives, as in the CRM patient journey: acquisition, conversion, adherence, and advocacy.

Typically, business rules are run in batch mode at a particular time of the day, or a particular day of the week. The results of these batch runs are lists generated for sending outbound communications, or lists of customers in the database that need to have their segment changed.

Campaign management software includes functionality for creating business rules, running rules, and generating lists. The software is typically tied directly to the CRM database, so that customer records can be accessed and updated. A partial list of such campaign management software is Alterian, Siebel, and Unica. The space is dynamic and for small CRM systems one can even develop a basic campaign management system using home-grown SQL or SAS code.

CAMPAIGN DATA TRANSMISSION

As we have illustrated throughout this book, members of both CRM and PRM programs are interacting with a manufacturer across multiple touch points. Indeed, they may be interacting with each other as part of social communities supported by the RM program. Furthermore, there is a benefit to storing summaries of these transactions in the RM database. This data transmission should be transmitted at least weekly, and daily if possible. For digital channels, including website and mobile, in principle data may be transmitted real time, going right to the database once the consumer submits.

The most critical data to be collected is the program registration and opt-in. Depending on the acquisition channel, this data transmission may be completely automated, or it may be partially manual. For example, handwritten BRCs must often be rekeyed by hand, or at least scanned with optical character recognition and checked manually. The same follows for contact information that is recorded on a telephone call interactive voice response (IVR) output. In terms of website registration forms, these are automatically stored in local data tables before a batch transmission to the RM database.

In the operational setup of a campaign, it is critical to insure consistency of data capture across communication channels. This is especially required for segment-based RM, where the segments are determined with a brief registration survey. Consider, for example, a Type 2 diabetes related program that aims to acquire patient members via a website, in-office brochures, printed BRCs and an automated phone IVR script. Say the website registration survey includes these two questions:

1. How long have you been diagnosed with Type 2 diabetes?

    a)   newly diagnosed

    b)   less than 6 months

    c)   6 months to 1 year

    d)   more than 1 year.

For question 1 above, the answers are in multiple-choice format where each is a time range. The time ranges should be compatible across channels. Most straightforwardly, the same multiple-choice options should be given on printed materials and on the phone.

Now say the BRC cannot fit the multiple choices of question 1, and instead asks a registrant:

1. How many months has it been since you were diagnosed with Type 2 diabetes? _____

Presumably, a registrant will write an integer zero or higher. In the consumer database, we want to store all consumers in this program together with compatible answers to the same questions. The multiple-choice and the integers are incompatible data types, which might be problematic for the database. Additionally, consider analyses or segmentation we may want to conduct based on this question. While the integers from the reply card can be aggregated to the multiple-choice ranges; the opposite is not true: the multiple-choice time ranges cannot be dissected any further to infer particular months. Thus, an analysis can show what percentage of the responders were diagnosed six to 12 months ago, but it cannot determine how many were diagnosed six to nine months ago, or exactly three months ago.

Consider another website registration survey question within the same diabetes program:

2.   What specialty of HCP is currently treating your diabetes?

a)   PCP

b)   endocrinologist

c)   certified diabetes educator

d)   other professional

A paper-based form, part of the in-office materials, may instead ask the question as a write-in:

2. What specialty of HCP is treating your diabetes? (enter below)

In this case the answer may be one of the choices from the website question, or it may be altogether different. The analysis could be very tricky. If a consumer enters "family practice" on the in-office form, then that could be grouped into the (a) PCP category from the website. However, if the consumer enters "nurse" then this may be ambiguous.

These incompatible survey types across channels may seem contrived, but they happen routinely. In part, this is because for some CRM programs there are distinct communication agencies developing the website and developing the printed materials, and perhaps yet another working on the call center scripting. When this occurs, it is essential to have an authorized campaign management leader who has responsibility to insure consistency.

FULFILLMENT AND COMPOSITION SPECIFICATION

Outbound communications within healthcare RM programs often consist of multiple elements all within the same package. This is especially true of direct mail packages such as a welcome kit or redemption of an offer, for example a complimentary blood pressure monitor from some promotional offer. Furthermore, the components may have alternate versions depending on the segment.

A fulfillment vendor must keep track of the alternate versions of outbound communications for each segment over time, to make sure that each RM member is receiving the appropriate materials. The documentation for keeping track of this is referred to as a "fulfillment code matrix," or alternatively a "kit code matrix." This matrix is merely a spreadsheet table, where each row specifies:

- a time range of applicability;

- a segment in the RM program;

- itemized components of what is included in the outbound package, including specific materials, versioned letters, and so on;

- amounts of monetized offers (relevant to over-the-counter or healthcare consumer packaged goods).

With the fulfillment code matrix in place, then the aforementioned business rules engine needs to place, in the right-hand side of the outbound communication rules, which fulfillment code is applicable for each segment and time.

THE CAMPAIGN MANAGEMENT PLAYBOOK

It's a great deal of effort to design an RM campaign, from the first brainstorming of business goals, to the user experience designs, through to the final creation of communication pieces and the media planning. It's critical not to let that careful thought go to waste as you are about to head into market.

The campaign management playbook is where all of the operational specifications sit in one well-structured document. The playbook includes the segmentation specifications and how segments are computed at registration time, or from the database. It maps out the communication plan by segment and the business rules for determining under what conditions each communication is sent. Also included are the fulfillment requirements for each communication and each testing plan.

The playbook should not be massive or burdensome; 20 to 50 pages is sufficient. This is the necessary script that all vendor partners must follow, so put time into a clear design.

Having this playbook is critical to insuring that when executed in-market, your RM program brings the consumers or HCPs the experience that was designed.

OPERATIONAL MONITORING AND TROUBLESHOOTING

Given the complexity of an in-market relationship marketing program, there is an ongoing need to insure the process is running smoothly at all components. This, indeed, is a measurement process in itself, akin to quality control on a factory floor. Each exchange of data between vendors and agencies should be validated for correct data types, timeliness, and quantities within a close range of forecasts.

The following should be in place in order to maintain operational control:

- Documentation is critical in all vendor agreements, promotional schedules, data exchanges, and forecasts. Both the lead RM agency and the manufacturer marketing client should have full transparency to all relevant information.

- Weekly operations calls with all vendors and agencies, including a delegate from the marketing client, should be scheduled, with a chance to review all checkpoints and raise any discrepancies.

- All measurable data streams should be plotted on a weekly chart and quantities trended over time to detect any anomalies. Indeed, this is a similar process to statistical process control (see Oakland 2008), where time series processes are carefully measured and alerts are generated when values are all above or below control limits.

Occasionally a CRM process will yield different results from the expected forecasts. This divergence may be due to one or more of the following.

- unusually high or low response rates to promotions;

- new marketplace events;

- delayed data gathering or data transfers;

- incorrect file encoding.

Whatever the cause, a rigorous monitoring process will detect such changes and identify any issues requiring resolution. Those issues need to be discussed with specialists across the different vendors and agencies, until a root cause is identified and a solution is implemented where necessary.

Exercises for Chapter 6

Question 6.1   For the media plan outlined at the end of Chapter 5 on the ABCOS CRM launch, what source coding and data transmission issues must be addressed?

Question 6.2   Design a simple contact stream of three communications for patient registrants of the ABCOS CRM program. Highlight any specific business rules that should be activated to trigger those contacts.

7

Measurement of Healthcare Relationship Marketing Programs

During the Measurement phase of relationship marketing (RM), we are assessing the impact of programs that are up and running in the marketplace. This chapter will first describe the purpose of measuring healthcare RM, and then proceed to itemize in detail the measurement of each phase of the campaign based on the patient journey, and the healthcare professional (HCP) journey.

We will also cover several special topics in this chapter:

- The use of visual, interactive performance dashboards for consumer relationship marketing (CRM) and professional relationship marketing (PRM).

- Specific ways to measure digital channels within pharmaceutical RM, such as "engagement."

- An industry expert interview as further perspective on digital analysis.

- Dedicated measurements that are particularly valuable to PRM, especially as related to understanding the interplay between personal (sales force) promotion and non-personal promotion (NPP).

The Various Measurement Objectives

Measurement of a CRM or PRM campaign has several objectives:

1.   *Business goal attainment*: determining whether the brand (or portfolio) communications goals are being achieved, as spelled out in the learning plan (discussed in the Strategy chapter of this book).

     This really means that we are measuring progress along the patient and the HCP journeys, as spelled out by the brand objectives. This means, for CRM, we measure whether our particular campaign is causing additional patients to convert to therapy, or we measure whether patients are becoming more adherent on the therapy. For PRM, we evaluate whether additional physicians are trying and adopting medication at increasing rates. For both CRM and PRM, we may measure advocacy, meaning:

     •   Are patients recommending this therapy to other patients, who in turn are converting to therapy?

     •   Are physicians acting influentially and encouraging their colleagues to also try the therapy on appropriate patients?

2.   *Optimization of promotional investments:* quantifying the number of direct response leads being generated from each media or other promotional source so that we can continually redirect our spending toward those media and promotional tactics that are driving qualified responders.

3.   *Operational monitoring*: assessing the operational functioning of the RM system to ensure information is flowing as expected,and there are no breakdowns in delivering on the multi-channel experience.

     For example, we measure the flow of traffic through a website, in part to insure that patients or HCPs are effectively finding the information they need and achieving goals like registration and access to tools. Additionally, we measure flow of leads from acquisition sources like website registrations, business reply cards (BRCs), or interactive voice responses (IVR), to insure that these response channels are successfully enabling registration.

4. *Campaign impact evaluation*: estimating the financial impact of a particular RM campaign by comparing the stream of incremental sales to the financial investments made in deploying the campaign.

We will now devote specific sections of this chapter to measurement and tracking techniques that support each of these objectives.

Industry Expert Perspective: Online Measurement in Pharmaceuticals

Digital channels are playing an increasing role in pharmaceutical marketing. Given this evolution, we need a methodology for measuring the impact of digital components and their utilization within a RM program.

For a perspective on the role of Internet-based metrics on pharmacetuical CRM, we have turned to industry veteran Mark Taylor, who is responsible for Interactive Marketing Operations at Rosetta. This group represents 350 people divided into four areas of inter-related expertise: Search; Online and Social Media; Relationship Marketing Technology; and Analytics/Optimization. Previously Mark has held leadership positions in digital marketing and technology at Wunderman, Young & Rubicam, EuroRSCG, and Le Mac et la Plume (within Havas).

Haimowitz: How can we best measure online behavior in pharmaceutical CRM, especially when patients are not directly purchasing online?

Taylor: Engagement metrics need to be established to indicate and illustrate what success looks like online for pharmaceutical marketers. Again, by building in utility and by using that utility to create trust, relevance, and exchange, you can create conversations with your consumers. The best engagement metrics will be found here.

Haimowitz: What is the role of an "online engagement" measurement framework within pharmaceutical consumer or professional RM?

Taylor: First and foremost, this needs to serve as a marketing discipline. An engagement framework should dictate the focus of pharmaceutical marketers online. It is crucial to develop and test proxies for consumer value. All testing of messaging, incentives, creative executions, and so on, should be intrinsically linked to the engagement framework.

Haimowitz: How can "online engagement" be made into a formal quantitative measurement that is a true leading indicator of eventual Rx conversion, or Rx adherence?

Taylor: Once the engagement metrics are established—the hypothesis that these are valid proxies for valuable behavior needs to be tested against real consumer or professional prescription data. Beyond the purely financial, there are metrics that should be measured and managed such as advocacy. Consider over-the-counter health categories like infant nutrition or diapers. How much is it worth that an "influential" mother blogs about the effectiveness of product X? That's testable. In-market tests will also help us develop that rigor.

Haimowitz: How rapidly is the pharmaceutical industry adopting new media channels in Consumer RM, such as mobile and social networks?

Taylor: The pharmaceutical industry has always been slow to adopt new channels. Mobile is crucial for them as it is the single best platform on which to deliver the mix of marketing and utility we have already discussed. We all understand the regulatory environment. But ensuring that the right people are at the table as we begin to think about new initiatives in new channels will help push the boundaries. Just being there of course is not enough, the marketers need to push and keep pushing to get beyond the inertia surrounding new approaches. Companies are starting to pull off some very interesting initiatives in the mobile and social spaces in particular. I expect this to be the catalyst for many more.

Defining Online Engagement

Mark Taylor's perspective in this interview is that digital channels are best measured with a quantitative online *engagement* metric system, that is ultimately verifiable through prescription data, or sales data in those health categories where purchase information may be available. However, this is a new concept, specifically used for digital channels, and the definition is not universally agreed upon.

By introducing some formalism, we can move toward possible definitions of engagement, and understand the alternatives.

Let $\mathbf{P_1}, \mathbf{P_2}, \ldots \mathbf{P_N}$ represent the N total possible touch points of a RM program, whether it is consumer or professional. These touch points may represent pages of a website, the opening or the clicking on an email of a mobile text, the opening of a direct mail, the placement of a phone call, or the return of a BRC or coupon.

Let $\mathbf{W_1}, \mathbf{W_2}, \ldots \mathbf{W_N}$ be numerical weights representing the weighted importance of each of the touch points in the RM program. For simplicity's sake, presume that the sum of all the $W_i = 1$. Alternatively, if you would rather design each weight to be on some other scale (such as from 1 to 5), then this is also permissible, for we will divide at the end by the sum of all weights.

For each participant within a the RM program, over a timespan T, let $\mathbf{I_1}, \mathbf{I_2}, \ldots \mathbf{I_N}$ be indicator variables that denote whether that member has in fact participated in each corresponding touch point during timespan T.

Ij = 1 if touch point j was consumed, and Ij = 0 if it was not consumed.

Then the engagement of that one member over the timespan T is defined as:

$$\sum_{j=1 \text{ to } N} I_j * W_j$$

$$\overline{\sum_{j=1 \text{ to } N} W_{jj}}$$

In other words, the engagement for that participant is the sum of the standardized weights of all the touch points that the CRM participant actually consumed, during that timespan. Then, the average engagement of the entire RM program is the same sum, over all participants. The author realizes that double indices could have been used, an extra index for the participant count, but wished to keep things simpler for the reader.

The alternative definitions of engagement stem from different definitions of the touch points and the weights:

- A *goal-based definition of* engagement is one where only a limited number of the weights have non-zero value, namely those that are in line with the goals of the program. Those touch points that are in line with the goals may have varying weights as well. Consider, for example, the branded website within a CRM program, and that we wish to measure the engagement related to acquisition. Then the website pages such as "talk to your doctor," "register for more information," or "screening questionnaire" may have positive weights, and everything else zero weight.

- A *time-based definition of engagement* may use as the weight the time spent on each touch point, or a zero weight if the touch point is not visited. The engagement then simplifies to the time spent on elements of the RM program.

- A *page view (or frequency) definition of engagement* is one where all of the weights are equal, and the engagement is essentially the number of touch points consumed.

- A *monetization definition of engagement* is similar to a goal-based definition, however the weights are actually estimates of the financial contribution that each touch point contributes to the overall business goal. This is especially used when measuring conversion (such as prescriptions or sales). These monetized weights should be derived based on a multivariate analysis from previous data.

Note that combinations of these definitions are also allowed. One may use as the weights the time spent on goal pages or the monetized value of the goal pages visited. For a more detailed discussion of web analytics incorporating engagement and monetitization, see Burby and Atkinson (2007). Ultimately, the takeaway is: if your company, or a consultant or agency you use, recommends using "engagement" as a measurement for awareness, acquisition, or conversion, then you should probe further and agree you are aligned as exactly how this measure of success is really being defined.

Generally speaking, the author feels that some kind of goal-based definition of engagement is most appropriate, provided that the goal-oriented touch points can be agreed upon. However, for the rest of this chapter, we will not take a stand on which definition of engagement should be used for each section of RM.

Once established, a weighted engagement calculation can be readily implemented within a web analytics tracking tool; some of the leading tools at the time of writing are Webtrends, Omniture, and Google Analytics. Implementation involves properly denoting or tagging the goal pages. Then, engagement may be tracked over time and by the media source that drove the visitors to the website. The resulting tracking table might appear as the example shown in Table 7.1:

Table 7.1 **Online media evaluation by engagement**

Media Source	Visitors	Average Time on Site (sec)	Average Page Views	Website (Goal-based) Engagement Score
Direct traffic				
Organic Search				
Paid Search				
Emails or Texts				
Banners				
Referrals				
Offline traffic				

Using this table, one can compare different media sources based on alternative measures of engagement. Let's step through a description of each of these media source categories:

- *Direct traffic:* these are website visitors that directly type in the URL, such as www.drugbrand.com, or use a bookmark after having previously visited. Most of this traffic may come due to offline, or in-office branding initiatives. Sometimes, somewhat controversially, direct traffic visits to a website are given credit as banner-related visits, if within a certain timespan.

- *Organic search:* these are from search engine results that are not paid advertisements and usually due to a high ranking on the top page.

- *Paid search*: these are sponsored search results which often appear at the top or side of a search engine page. These visitors come as a result of a paid search campaign.

- *Emails or texts*: visitors that click on an opened email or text message and come to a website.

- *Banners:* visitors coming after a click on a banner advertisement. As mentioned above, website analytics software count this as instant linkage, yet some media tracking tools use cookie tracking to include those clicks occurring after viewing a banner in the recent past (such as 30 days ago or less).

- *Referrals*: visitors that come from another website which includes a link to this website. This can be an excellent source of leads to investigate, for it may include potential partner organizations for a manufacturer.

- *Offline traffic*: these are visitors coming as a result of a call to action from a non-digital source, such as a print ad, a medical convention, or an out-of-door advertisement, that made use of a dedicated (or "vanity") URL for tracking that source to the website.

Note that direct marketing best practice usually advises that media elements do not link to a website's homepage but rather to a landing page that continues the customer experience from the source, and often that encourages registration in the RM program.

In fact, an alternative version of the table, shown in Table 7.2, can also be calculated that explicitly computes the number of engaged visitors, and the cost per engaged visitor.

While these tables are at the aggregate media levels, they may be broken down at further levels of detailed media locations, or even testing elements (creative, offers, and so on). Their calculation is all dependent on proper source coding and tagging, which has been described in detail in Chapter 6.

Table 7.2   Online media evaluation combining cost and engagement

Media Source	Cost for Media	Engaged Visitors	Cost per Engaged Visitor
Direct traffic			
Organic Search			
Paid Search			
Emails or Texts			
Banners			
Referrals			
Offline traffic			

Website Path Analysis

For many RM programs, a website is the hub of the activity. Therefore one crucial component of measuring engagement is understanding the behaviors of visitors to the RM website. Figure 7.1 demonstrates a basic path analysis of visitors coming to the hypothetical consumer website of the fictitious osteoporosis drug ABCOS from ABC Pharmaceuticals. The layout of the website is typical, although there is no intentional resemblance to any actual product website in particular.

This analysis superimposes on the home page of the website the probabilities of which link the visitor will click on after arrival on the home page. At the top left of the analysis is noted the *abandon rate,* which is the percentages of visitors that leave the website altogether after arriving at this home page. An abandon rate of 30 percent, as noted in the figure, is within the typical range for pharmaceutical branded product websites. Then, for all other content areas of the website, the percentages next to each area are the empirical probability of a visitor next clicking on that section.

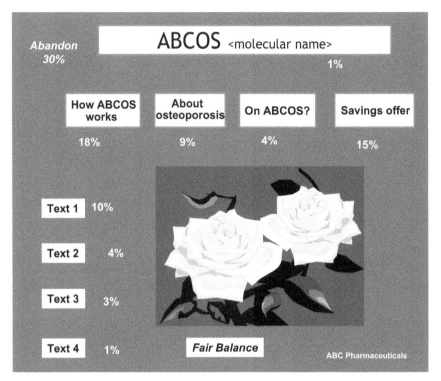

Figure 7.1   Website path analysis

Examining these percentages, a few patterns become evident. Because (in English-speaking countries) people read from left to right, there is usually a pattern of decreasing click likelihoods when moving from left to right. This certainly holds for the sections at the top of the ABCOS website, with one exception: the savings offer, all the way to the right of the page, actually has a high percentage, due to strong consumer interest. Another pattern that usually holds is that percentages decrease from top to bottom. This can be seen to hold for the listings "Text 1" to "Text 4" (the true website would have names filled in) on the left-hand side.

This is known as a *one click path analysis*, because we are measuring only what happens on the first click from the home page. It is recommended to at least perform a two click path analysis for the most highly visited areas.

There are other variations on this home page path analysis. For direct response channels that drive to a landing page, which is recommended, these percentages can be evaluated from the landing page. As we will discuss later this chapter, a full path funnel analysis should be performed for the intended path visitors are to take through the RM registration process. Another point worth noting: the analyses above can also be completed by source of leads, to determine the details of the behavior for each source.

Measuring Improvement in Awareness

Typically, increasing brand or portfolio awareness is not a primary objective of a RM program. However, any significant promotional program with a wide visibility may have a brand awareness impact and this is worth measuring.

The simplest, "on faith" measurement of the awareness impact is estimating the total impressions or circulation of the promotional media. Generally speaking, it is true that increased aggregate impressions often lead to increased awareness, until a saturation point is reached. However, mere impression counting is not directly quantifiable for assessing the brand impact, because not all those "exposed" to the media may have an increased brand awareness or favorable impression.

A much more effective way to assess awareness is through primary market research surveys, alternately called "Brand Awareness" studies, or "Awareness, Trial, and Usage" (ATU) studies. These analyses are conducted over time, on a rotating cross section within the target segment population. For example, for our running case study on ABC Pharmaceuticals and the ABCOS osteoporosis product, the survey may be conducted quarterly on a rotating sample of post-menopausal women aged over 55. By holding this survey over time, one can assess the lift in awareness due to an advertising promotion, including CRM.

The questions asked in the ATU study usually fall into three categories:

1. *Brand Awareness*: this line of questioning quantifies answers to: Is the promotion getting noticed? Is it being associated with our brand in some manner? Are consumers aware of our brand?

2. *Brand attributes*: this series of questions is asked to assess: Are the promotional materials conveying the intended product attributes? Is the product (or company) differentiated versus the competition? What does the product, or company, as a brand stand for with customers (either consumers or HCPs)?

3. *Call to action*: this section of questions measures whether the in-market promotion has increased likelihood of action. For a consumer, questions would probe on an intent to visit the doctor and inquire about this treatment. For a physician, questions would probe regarding the likelihood of prescribing this product for appropriate patients. Of the three types of questions, this section specifically may be considered a measurement of the acquisition lift of the CRM program.

If the ATU study is indeed administered periodically over time, then a comparison can be made in ATU percentage questions from before and after a promotional campaign, including CRM. Thus if 15 per cent of target consumers were aware of the fictitious product ABCOS before the CRM campaign, and afterwards 25 percent are aware, and that difference is statistically significant based on sample size, we can presume an increase in ABCOS brand awareness due to the CRM campaign. Note this implicitly assumes there were no other major advertising or public relations initiatives taking place. Similarly, a significant positive difference in percentages on call to action questions, such as "likelihood to ask physician about ABCOS," can be counted as evidence of a positive acquisition effect.

Finally, given our articulation of engagement from earlier in this chapter, it is worth noting that awareness can also be measured using a digital engagement framework. If certain website pages, banner ads, or emails or text messages are intended to have a brand awareness impact, then touch points may be given positive weights in an awareness engagement calculation. This can readily be implemented within website analytics tools and broken out by promotional source as well.

Measuring Acquisition

From a RM perspective, acquisition means registration of members into the program database, so they may be contacted with further communications, offers, and support. Acquisition for a RM program is closely aligned with media planning and channel planning. The quantitative objectives for acquisition are typically:

1. register high volumes of qualified leads into a CRM database, to communicate with them about a disease condition or a specific treatment;

2.   do so efficiently, by minimizing the cost per qualified lead (CPQL).

Let's discuss how to quantifiably measure against each of these objectives for an acquisition campaign. Consider the selection criteria for the acquisition media mix. As discussed in our chapter on Strategy (Chapter 4), the media tactics chosen for a CRM program are based on meeting the target segments at significant decision points of the patient journey. There may be a whole set of media that satisfy those criteria, and so the CRM designer should take an approach of continual optimization based on volume and efficiency.

The primary metric to optimize is *cost per (unique) qualified lead,* which we shall abbreviate as CPQL. A careful definition of this term is required. Let's proceed step by step:

- A *lead* is a unique consumer who registers for the RM program.

  Note the emphasis on uniqueness. For a multichannel program, realistically, up to 10 percent of responders may be duplicates. This may be due to repeated submissions within the same channel (such as a website), or responses by the same consumer across multiple channels (say the IVR phone response as well as the website or BRC).

  It is critical for a CRM database vendor to utilize de-duplication software to reduce the list of responders to uniques. This software typically filters out duplicates via a combination of name and address matching algorithms.

- A *qualified lead* is a re-contactable responder who is a member of a target segment.

Two important concepts are emphasized here. First, re-contactable means that the consumers have supplied valid re-contact information: postal address, email address, or perhaps mobile number for texting. It also means that the consumers have explicitly opted-in to receive follow-up communications.

Second, qualified leads should be members of a target segment. The target segment was defined in the RM strategy development (see Chapter 4). For example, if a RM program is aimed at pain relief patients who are treating with over-the-counter medications, that can be determined by survey questions on the registration form. Therefore, in an operational setting, one can measure unique qualified leads for each in-market tactic that drives CRM acquisition.

After a certain time period, one can create a table such as Table 7.3 below which compares acquisition media tactics based on efficiency of generating qualified leads:

Table 7.3   Cost per qualified lead table

Media Source	Media Cost	Impressions / Circulation	Registration Rate	Unique, Qualified	Cost per Qualified Lead
DRTV					
DR Print					
Direct mail					
Emails or Texts					
Organic Search					
Paid Search					
Banners					
Referrals					

Again, as with the earlier tables presented in this chapter, one can include specific promotional tactics, or alternatives within an in-market test.

By definition, there are two components that make up the calculation of an efficient CPQL lead acquisition campaign:

1.   high response rate, among qualified targets;

2.   an effective registration process for those that respond.

The response rate (1) can be judged as successful based on prior experience within that channel, an assessment which can be made by a media company or direct marketing consultants. One can also consult a reference guide like the Direct Marketing Association (DMA) response rate book (DMA 2009).

The effective registration process can be evaluated through a funnel analysis, which is illustrated in Figure 7.2. This figure represents a typical sequence of actions that a website visitor must click through in order to become a registered member of a RM program. Numerical quantities are for illustration only, and are simplified for the purpose of this discussion.

- At the top of the funnel is the total visitors at the landing page, which hypothetically is given at 100,000 visitors per month.

- The next step is to reach a page describing the background and benefits of joining the RM program. As depicted in the figure, only 10.7 percent of landing page visitors make it there, meaning that 89.3 percent "drop off" the registration path. When this ratio is low, it can be that the callout on the landing page to register is unclear, or the value exchange is not compelling or clearly stated.

- The subsequent step is making it to the registration form page, where contact information is gathered, the visitor opts-in to receive communications, and a few survey questions are answered. In our

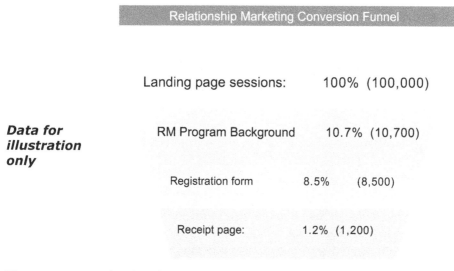

Figure 7.2   Evaluating the acquisition funnel

example within the figure, 8,500 of visitors make it to the registration form, which is 8.5 percent of the total visitors, and 79 percent of those from the previous step. When this ratio is low, it may be that prospects do not see the value of this program. However, in our example, 79 percent is quite a high ratio.

- Finally, the last step in the funnel is a receipt page that comes after the form is completed and the registration is submitted and accepted. In our example, 1,200 visitors complete the registration and get a receipt, which is 1.2 percent of the total visitors, and 14 percent from the previous step. When this figure is low, it may signify an overly complex registration form process, or survey questions that prospects do not wish to answer.

Funnels are not restricted to registrations within websites. They are also applicable to telephone responses. For an IVR system, there is a series of push-button menu items that must be followed in order to register for a program. Just as in Figure 7.1, callers drop off at every voice response that must be given, and this is tracked by different call centers for quality control and to measure effectiveness. For phone responses where live agents are employed, there is a script that the agents follow and data entry the agents must complete. Each of these can be tracked for status and completion.

Dashboards for Tracking Relationship Marketing Acquisition Responses

Given the nature of RM programs, there is a tendency to have a proliferation of tracking reports and associated spreadsheets, all emanating from different sources. Some reports may count registration by source, others may give impressions and click through rates of digital media, others may have financial spreadsheets of program costs, and still other reports may contain prescription impact. Furthermore, it may be that these different tabular reports arrive at different times of the month, making integration and company decision making nearly untenable.

To avoid the indecision that can result from a collection of disjointed tabular reports, it is most beneficial to create an integrated dashboard that visually depicts multi-faceted reports over an extended period of time. The dashboard should be able to handle dynamic queries and allow filtering for specific business questions and scenarios. We will show a few such dashboards in this section of the chapter. These dashboards were all implemented in Spotfire, a TIBCO software product.

RELATIONSHIP MARKETING RESPONSES BY MEDIA SOURCE VERSUS FORECAST

Figure 7.3 overleaf shows a dashboard used for evaluating and optimizing the marketing performance of a multi-channel RM campaign. Presume that this is a program which has been taking place during 2010 and is continuing into 2011. The first component is incorporating the forecast of responses that are expected throughout the new year of 2011. As mentioned in a previous chapter, this forecast can be made based on the expected response rates from individual tactics within the new 2011 media plan. In the figure, these response levels are shown on a month by month basis. Using the interactive data visualization tools, we build a drilldown component so that as a time interval within the forecast is highlighted in the upper panel, the monthly responses by media source appear in the lower panel. We see in the forecast by media source that the major media categories are print, online, direct mail, pharmacy, and events (such as public health fairs and screenings).

Within this dashboard, the forecast window can accommodate multiple time series. Let's overlay within this top panel a second time series: last year's actual responses. In a similar way to the forecast, by drilling down on last year's actual cumulative response curve, one can view monthly responses by media source. Notice that the 2011 forecast is projected to be larger than the 2010 forecast. A selection of both forecasts in the upper panel would demonstrate that the 2010 contribution from certain media sources is projected to increase.

Finally, we can overlay a third curve above, denoting the actual responses received thus far. So, if we have now collected responses through February of 2011, and our annual actual response curve has two monthly points. As shown in Figure 7.3, we are currently ahead of this year's forecast. Using drilldown, in the upper panel we select January through March of both this year's forecast and this year's actual, and find in the lower panel that for February both print and online responses were higher than the forecast predicted. This led to the overall higher response total in February. online responses have been higher than forecasted in March. Viewing the responses by media subcategory rather than just overall category, we might find, for instance, that a rise in Google paid search over the last year has been the primary performance difference.

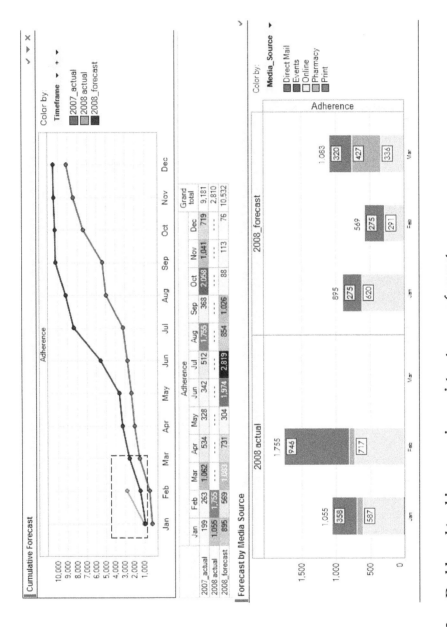

Figure 7.3 Dashboard tracking campaign registrants versus forecast

The filter capability of Spotfire allows us to show particular sections of these cumulative response curves. Using the check box filter on the timeframes, we can determine which curve we want to see, for highlighting differences either among forecasts or the actual responses. Using a slidebar filter of the months, we can select particular periods of time, either to highlight a difference, or to focus on recent months only.

Once a particular insight has been found, it should be captured and annotated, and within a dashboard there are several ways to do this. Most traditionally is making a screen capture of the trend or exception and pasting into a presentation program like Microsoft Power Point, where additional text can be typed.

Alternatively, the analytical insight can be "bookmarked" right within the dashboard. This means a text area can be added to the display, as a "margin" of commentaries on key insights This text can be hyperlinked to automatically recall links to the particular filter settings and displays found in Figure 7.3. Thus, no matter where we may be in the dashboard, selecting that text link brings us back to the insightful display. Over time, as one analyses the latest monthly data, and finds many insights, this margin of insight notations becomes populated with multiple bullets of hyperlinked text, a kind of executive summary with visual displays to match.

Dashboard supporting cost per qualified lead analysis

Figure 7.4 shows a view of how a dashboard can help us to optimize among a set of media properties within the same media channel, over time. The figure illustrates a set of advertisements for the same product, within various print publications, placed over the past two years, and organized by quarter. The upper panel shows average CPQL levels across the different media subcategories. As would be befitting of a category like osteoporosis for our running case of ABCOS, the print subcategories include African American, Women's Service, Women's Lifestyle, Health, Mature, and Shelter. CPQL varies among these categories, and is at its highest in the Women's Lifestyle category during Q2 and Q3. Note that a MANOVA statistical analysis could determine whether these differences are significant by season and/or by print category.

Using a drilldown we can see more details in the lower panel regarding the cost effectiveness of particular media tactics. For example, as illustrated in the figure, say a dashboard user wants to dig more deeply into the shelter

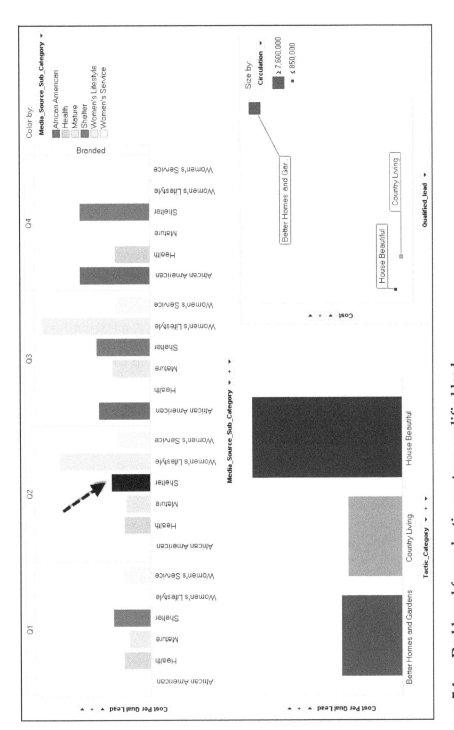

Figure 7.4   Dashboard for evaluating cost per qualified lead

category during the second quarter. By clicking on this bar of Shelter in Q2, what appears on the lower left are the specific CPQL figures for Better Homes and Gardens, Country Living, and House Beautiful. The outlier appears to be House Beautiful, with a very high CPQL. Numbers have been hidden for privacy. The panel at the lower right gives detail as to why House Beautiful has a particularly high CPQL in this case: a mid-range cost of the three publications, but a very low count of qualified leads.

Note that, typically, direct response print advertisements include a BRC for response, but they may also include multiple-response mechanisms, including a toll-free number leading to an IVR system, and a website landing page URL. The response levels by reply channel can also be a valuable dashboard display for tracking, for this can assist with resource planning of call centers.

Dashboard evaluating traffic source engagement

Another type of dashboard is quite valuable for detecting at a glance which sources of traffic are most valuable from an engagement standpoint. As shown in Figure 7.5 overleaf, this is a scatterplot diagram of various online traffic sources to a Product.com branded website. The X axis denotes the percentage of visitors from that source that visited a critical goal page, in this case the CRM overview page, which describes the benefits of registering. The Y axis describes the average number of website pages viewed by visitors from that source, which is a broad engagement metric.

A quadrant analysis is set up to assess the quality of leads from the various sources. The dashed lines, horizontal and vertical, represent the average measures for all visitors to the website. Therefore, those website traffic sources in the upper right quadrant are associated with particularly *highly engaged* visitors. Those in the lower right quadrant are *program driven*, in that they seek the CRM program page without doing much page navigation beforehand. Those sources in the upper right quadrant may be called *browsers*, in that the visitors traverse many pages yet do not seek out the CRM program. Finally, those sources in the lower left have visitors with low engagement.

What actions can be taken as a result of this dashboard? For one, promotions and media may be optimized to give preference to the highly engaged and the program-driven sources of leads, and to steer investments away from the lower right. For those sources sending browsers to the website, perhaps a stronger call to action can be given within the promotions (such as banners) for that source.

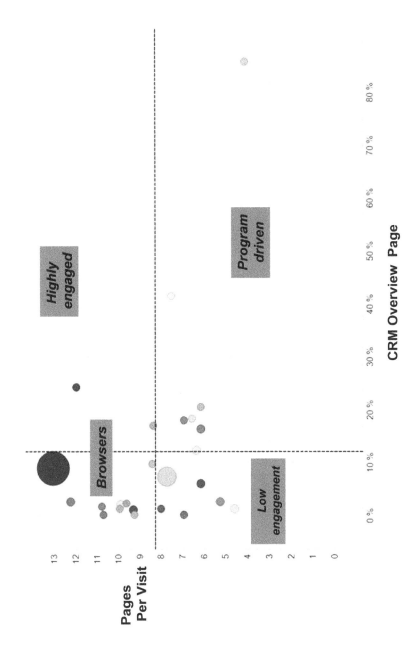

Note: Dotted lines indicate overall website average; Size of circle is # of visitors

Figure 7.5 Dashboard evaluating sources of referral traffic

This dashboard framework in Figure 7.5 can be presented with any category of website traffic sources, including referrals, email responses, search terms, and specific banner executions.

There are assumptions and caveats associated with these dashboards that are worth pointing out. One implicit assumption is that a campaign registrant can be ascribed to precisely one promotional source. In reality, a RM prospect may have viewed multiple media sources, even if taking action on just one of these. Another caveat is the need to wait for the promotion response curve to take effect. For example, if print publications take up to a year or more to obtain most responses, then the most recent time period will always have an unusually high CPQL. This is not a concern for channels with a faster response curve, including digital.

Direct Response Email Campaign Analysis

Direct emails are ideally measured with two components:

- the open rate, defined as the percentage of email recipients that open the email;

- the click through rate, defined as the percentage of opened emails from which the reader clicks through to the website.

A successful direct email campaign may have a 15 to 25 percent open rate amongst a targeted list, and then a 20 to 40 percent click through rate for those who have opened. Combining these results in a 3 to 10 percent email response rate, which would be an input rate before the website funnel takes effect. The analysis should be completed by determining the engagement and registration funnels associated with website visitors from the emails.

This two-phase response analysis also replies to text messages and personal digital assistant (PDA) messages. Thus, whether it is acquiring consumers with acquisition offers in the pharmacy, or educating professionals with Epocrates Doc Alerts, the same principles apply.

Email campaigns are also a prime opportunity to perform in-market tests. The following can and should be tested to determine optimal response rate:

- alternate subject line wording;

- alternate call to action, or value proposition wording;

- alternate placement of call to action within message;

- variations in use of imagery

Evaluating Patient Conversion

For pharmaceutical products, measuring the effect on conversion means comparing the incremental prescriptions among RM members versus those of a matched control group.

The standard practice has become a partnership with a Health Insurance Portability and Accountability Act (HIPAA)-compliant data provider of retail prescription data or other pharmaceutical claims data.

Such a vendor can take the set of registrants for a CRM program and determine their prescription activity within the category before and after the registration into the CRM program. The vendor can also select a matched control group to the CRM members, based on pair wise similarity of age, gender, geography, and recent medication history.

The evaluation of conversion is illustrated in Figure 7.6. Both populations are evaluated monthly over time, to see the rate at which each population begins on the CRM medication. In the figure, the evaluation is made at 180 days post CRM registration, and a similar 180 days since each paired control sample is obtained.

If the CRM member group converts at a statistically significant higher rate than the control group, then that is a positive result for the CRM program. In the case of the figure, there is a significant difference of 19.7 percent versus 2.6 percent conversion to drug.

Then, the difference in conversion rates versus control can be used as a parameter in an incremental sales calculation. Call this difference in conversion rates R_d (a percentage less than 1), and say N people have registered for the program. Then the estimated conversion impact of the program is $N * R_d * L$,

- Did the <u>lead generation</u> responders <u>convert</u> to your Rx more than a control group matched by age, gender, condition?

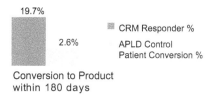

Figure 7.6   **Evaluating consumer relationship marketing: patient incremental conversion**

where L is the estimated lifetime value to the manufacturer of new patients beginning therapy. Say in our example from Figure 7.6 that 50,000 people had registered for the program, $R_d = 17.1\%$ (by calculation), and the lifetime value of a new patient is $500. Then the estimated conversion impact is:

$$50,000 * 17.1\% * \$500 = \$4,275,000.$$

Evaluating Lift in Patient Adherence

To evaluate the effect of a CRM program on patient adherence, one also uses a relative measure. As with the measurement of conversion, the evaluation is usually made by comparing the CRM registrants with a matched control group. In this case, both the CRM population and the control group are already patients on the CRM-related treatment, and the control group matched patients should have started therapy at the same time. This is illustrated in Figure 7.7.

The analysis measures incremental treatments at monthly time intervals, aiming to answer the following question:

- After M months on therapy, what is the incremental average number of medication doses of the CRM member group versus the control group?

If there is a significant difference between the CRM member group and the control group, then it may be worthwhile to investigate which of the two components is more influential in this difference: a change in compliance (taking medication regularly, as directed), or a change in persistence (taking medication over time). The compliance is measured by examining the frequencies of refills (for the more

- Did the <u>adherence</u> <u>program</u> responding patients <u>take more medicine over time</u> than a matched control group of other patients?

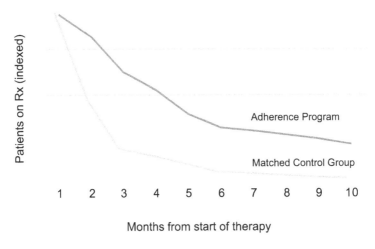

Figure 7.7   Tracking adherence of CRM responders

medication is skipped, the later the refills are made), whereas the persistence comparing the frequency of refills. A business rule needs to be established, if there is no refill for N months (N may be 3), that patient is deemed off therapy, and the persistence lasted until the last refill would have been used up.

In Chapter 3, in the section "Sales Forecasts in the Therapeutic Category," we mapped out a calculation of patient persistence and compliance, and how to combine these into a lifetime value calculation. The reader is asked to review this section for understanding the relationship among these concepts.

To determine the overall impact of incremental adherence for a CRM program, multiply the incremental lifetime value for patients, times the number of patients who join the CRM program on therapy, and engage with the adherence activities of the CRM program.

Measuring Consumer Relationship Marketing Patient Advocacy

Patient advocacy refers to when patients who have a positive experience with a treatment then share their experiences. The implementation of advocacy components is evolving and experimental, and therefore there is no standard approach to measurement.

Within the growing and changing social media landscape, patients share their healthcare experiences routinely and to different extents depending on the therapeutic category. Therefore, social media scraping and analysis, with sentiment assessments if possible, is a valuable tracking tool. The challenge is not knowing exactly which consumers posting where associated with the CRM program itself. To manage this challenge, one may:

- attempt a before and after comparison to detect changes in levels after the CRM program is implemented;

- implement a kind of community within the CRM program itself, for members to share news in the category. This has been successfully implemented for non-pharmaceutical health and wellness brands.

There can also be room for other activity tracking of more structured "pass along" initiatives. Websites, emails, or even direct mail, can be appropriately coded, and clicks, open rates or mail-ins can be counted.

We have just enumerated the various measurements for the performance of CRM. In the sections that follow, we will step through the corresponding measurements for PRM, especially taking note of what is distinctive.

Measuring Healthcare Professional Awareness and Engagement for Professional Relationship Marketing

For PRM, impact on awareness can be measured in much the same way as discussed for consumers in the section "Measuring Improvement in Awareness" above. ATU market research tracking studies are often fielded to gauge physicians' opinions of pharmaceutical products and the sales forces of healthcare companies. These can be extended to ask HCPs if they have participated in, or are aware of, the PRM program as well, and that can form a cohort for comparisons.

Somewhat related to awareness research is tracking whether PRM, and the services offered to professionals, has improved the reputation of a manufacturer as a partner and a provider of value to HCPs. Two or three questions appended to ATU surveys, or even a dedicated survey within the PRM program, can be quite valuable.

Regarding engagement, the definitions we have developed in the section "Defining Online Engagement" above are also applicable, particularly as non-personal promotion expands into digital channels. For PRM, however, engagement is not a merely a single number, but rather an assessment of which types of information and services the HCPs find most valuable. Engagement is multifaceted, and we track engagement along these dimensions:

- *Product related*: are the professionals spending time learning about product attributes and benefits, and related clinical data?

- *Professional education*: are professionals learning about the state of the art, and innovations in the therapeutic category from key opinion leaders (KOLs)?

- *Practice resources*: to what extent are professionals accessing content to train their staff, publicize their practice, or improve the administrative efficiency of their office?

- *Patient education:* are professionals leveraging PRM to obtain better educational materials for their patients?

- *Sales linkage:* is PRM being utilized to request samples, requesting a sales representative visit, or even making a direct purchase (where appropriate)?

Note that comprehensive assessment of HCP engagement requires analytics from multiple channels, including data integration, across multiple touch points within an integrated professional database. The benefit of tracking engagement by category and across channels is obtaining the feedback on which services are found most valuable to targeted HCPs. Then services can be improved and customized, and the value can be reinforced by the sales force. We will speak in more depth about measuring the feedback loop later in this chapter.

Measuring Healthcare Professional Acquisition for Professional Relationship Marketing

Acquisition for PRM is directly analogous as to the consumer side: the objective is still to register individuals as program members into the database. There is still a benefit to examining all acquisition funnel pathways, usually website or phone, for smooth operations and effectiveness. Also, as with CRM, there is indeed a benefit to reviewing all promotional channels for how efficiently they generate qualified leads into the database.

Some distinctions do arise in evaluating acquisition for HCPs. One is the notion of what constitutes a *qualified lead*. As with consumers, we do want to insure uniqueness and have reliable contact information, either postal address and/or email address. For professionals, there is also an issue of prescriber validation, insuring that the registrant is in fact a licensed professional and, where possible, also validating this professional is authorized to prescribe medications. The validation can take place by requesting a state license number at registration, or other identification. Some PRM systems also follow up with a phone call to the HCP's office to verify contact information and credentials. Note that for PRM there may be members who are not prescribing physicians, such as certified diabetes educators or office staff. However, validation is recommended even for these individuals. Also, the designation of a "qualified" lead may include other criteria such as:

- being in a particular professional specialty;

- being affiliated with a certain type of institution, such as integrated delivery systems, hospital network, or a physician network;

- being an active prescriber in the relevant therapeutic category.

Satisfaction of any such additional conditions can be determined using a match to American Medical Association (AMA) or related professional demographic files, as well as using physician-level prescribing data or account-level sales data.

Another intrinsic distinction in PRM acquisition arises due to the element of personal promotion by the sales force. As we discussed back in Chapter 2, the sales representatives may be promoting the PRM system through leave-behind materials, or through slides on the tablet PC presentations. The field force may also be able to register professionals into the PRM program, either within an office setting or at a medical convention. Whatever combination of these is in place, it is worth evaluating the personal promotional channel on its effectiveness of enabling acquisition of qualified leads into PRM programs.

Evaluating Professional Relationship Marketing Trial and Adoption

Measuring the impact of PRM on HCP trial and adoption entails comparing the prescribing or purchase trends of PRM members with the trends of a matched control group. The control group of professionals should be matched to the PRM member groups by geography, specialty, prescribing deciles in the relevant therapeutic categories, and coverage by pharmaceutical sales forces. In addition, members of the control group should not be members of the same group practice as any member of the PRM "test" group.

Depending on the therapeutic category and the enrollees, doctor-level prescription data may not be appropriate. For hospitals, long-term care centers, or federal institutions, account-level sales data can be used. For members who are not actual prescribers, then self-reported surveys can be used, granted similar surveys exist on a control group.

The analysis can compare a positive impact of the PRM platform on prescribing when:

- there is a trend in increasing product sales after the PRM registration versus before; and

- that trend is a steeper increase than the control group of non-registered PRM attendees.

- (Note that in the rare case the prescribed treatment is actually losing prescriptions, and PRM may in fact stem that loss, that is also a positive impact on prescribing.)

In particular, for a treatment early in its lifecycle, the PRM program impacts trial when a larger percentage of physicians in the PRM group write the drug for the first time. Similarly, the PRM program impacts adoption if a larger percentage in the PRM group attain a certain market share than the control group (this threshold share can be agreed upon in the learning plan, say half the overall market share).

In addition, there are some leading indicators that may be part of a PRM portal website, which can be measured to gauge leading indicators of eventual product trial or adoption. These include requesting a sample, requesting a sales representative visit, perhaps even checking formulary status. These are all click-stream transaction activities that can be measured and assigned to logged-in visitors to PRM.

Special Professional Relationship Marketing Analyses on Promotional Channels

PRM is particularly fascinating as a measurement system because it combines innovation in both personal and non-personal promotion, as well as presenting feedback loops between these two classes of channels. This naturally leads to four lines of analysis:

1. What is the impact of sales force innovation (interactive tablets or PDAs) on selling and what new information can be gathered about the HCPs?

2. How do HCPs engage within the non-personal channels, which are dispersed and increasingly digital?

3. How do the personal and non-personal channels complement or compete with each other for the promotional attention of the HCP?

4. How effective is the feedback loop that can link these channels, in either direction:

    • how can sales representatives adapt their messaging-based information about the HCP's non-personal activities;

    • how can NPPs (especially digital) and portals be adapted based on what is presented by sales representatives on their tablets?

Note that question (2) above was really handled earlier in our formal treatment of "engagement." We shall describe approaches to answering the other categories of questions within the rest of this section.

MULTI-FACETED MEASUREMENT IS REQUIRED

Before proceeding with specifics, it is worth noting that evaluation of any aspect of PRM effectiveness requires a multi-faceted approach to measurement, as illustrated in Figure 7.8; there has to be integration of data, and of insights across:

- primary research conducted on both the HCPs as well as the sales force representatives;

- secondary audit data with demographics, as well as prescription behaviors. Both of these can form the basis of segmentation, and prescription behavior of course forms the basis of outcome metrics;

- in-market channel interactions, whether from the sales force tablet activities or interactions that professionals have with interactive touch points.

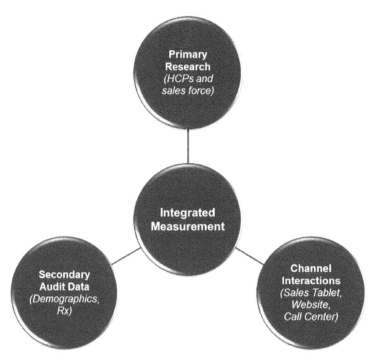

Figure 7.8   **Professional relationship marketing requires an integrated measurement approach**

PRM value is measured across channels and by segment. The ultimate goal is not to measure PRM value in isolation. The measurement can be made by segment for additional perspective. Additionally, these PRM value metrics should be merged with prescribing data to calculate return on investment (ROI), and to optimize channels and messages by segment.

Each PRM analysis is enabled by an integrated professional data warehouse. As mentioned in Chapter 6, the manufacturer's professional core master system typically needs to be extended from one primarily supporting sales force call-sample-detail activity to a more complete repository that stores an expanded set of time-stamped transactions across all marketing touch points with HCPs.

OPTIMIZING THE TABLET PC SALES PRESENTATIONS

Many pharmaceutical companies are now selling with digital tablets, where almost every click the sales representative makes can be measured and time tabulated. These tablets generate sequential data streams, which are sometimes measured with elementary metrics such as time spent and the order of tablet slides used.

This is reminiscent of the early days of website analytics around the year 2000, where the metrics often cited were page views and time on website. Back then, those were used as key performance indicators (KPIs) because they were reportable in the elementary "web log" systems.

However, the objective of selling with sales tablets should be to achieve a business goal. Just as we now use goal-oriented measurement for websites, like RM registration, do the same for your tablets. Think about your brand objectives and what particular sections of the tablet presentations are most aligned toward achieving those goals. Measure consumption of those sections as a valuable indicator of success.

Because analysis of tablet PC sales presentations holds many similarities with website behavior analysis, as both are a form of path analysis, certain measurements are naturally relevant:

- Frequency and percentage of sales presentations resulting in presentation of goal-oriented content. This is a subset of general frequency distributions. Either way, as a result, some slides may be reconsidered due to low visibility or shifted to another place in the presentation.

- The sequences of visual aids presented are analyzed against those sequences practiced at plan of actions sales meeting (POA) training. That role play may be viewed as reinforcing an experience map of the interaction between two personas: that of the sales representative and that of the HCP.

- Certain sequences may be viewed as a "funnel," making it valuable to measure how often is the sequence completed, is the "goal view" of key product content reached during the call, and if not, where is the drop-off, due to lack of time, or distractions?

Each of these analyses can be conducted by physician segment as, typically, pharmaceutical companies intend to deliver somewhat tailored messaging by segment.

INTERACTION BETWEEN THE HEALTHCARE PROFESSIONAL PROMOTIONAL CHANNELS

In this general topic area, a healthcare marketing and sales organization wants to understand how the personal and non-personal promotional channels complement each other. The specific business questions to be answered can be categorized as follows:

Reach:

- Who are the HCPs that are taking advantage of the non-personal channels within PRM?

- How do these professionals compare to the called-on targeted physicians of the sales force?

- Is the reach of contacted professionals expanded due to PRM? That is, are "no see" and lower priority professionals now being serviced with PRM?

Frequency:

- How often are professionals returning to the non-personal elements of PRM?

- Is the frequency of contacts increasing to the professionals already called on by the sales force?

Promotion response analysis:

- Consider a non-personal promotional "call" any of the following: response to a direct mail piece, opening and click through of an email, an e-detail, a text message alert, or a website portal interaction. Do each of these non-personal calls result in an extension of the promotion response curve?

- For HCPs not called on by sales forces, what is the shape of the purely non-personal response curve compared to the sales force promotion response?

- Is NPP as cost effective, and as impactful, as a sales force call? If not, what weighting applies?

Any of these questions can become an analytics project in its own right. The critical precursor is to merge information from the different promotional channels to the same HCPs into a single time-ordered sequence. Then special categories of time series analysis will apply (see Wei 2005); one may think of a multivariate time series to account for the different channels.

IMPLEMENTING AND MEASURING THE FEEDBACK LOOP

Closed loop marketing (CLM) is an often-stated objective for continually improving professional promotion and for tailoring the communications to specific customers. We feel this is achievable by implementing business rules found in all RM programs. In particular, the business rules needed for PRM map the professional segment and the individual's PRM value to future communications.

For example, recall the three-tiered segmentation approach that we developed in our Chapter 4 on Strategy. Say a Tier one professional is called upon by the sales representative, who delivers an effective product message via tablet PC, and also directs the physician to register on the website portal and view a KOL video. After this physician performs these activities on the health portal, a notification is sent back to the sales representative, who can follow-up on the next call, continue the dialogue related to the KOL video, and ask the physician if they have any questions.

Furthermore, marketing headquarters is notified (in summary reports) as to which segments of HCPs are viewing the KOL videos, and which sales aids on the representatives' tablets are most effectively used in sales calls.

What this example demonstrates is that multiple stakeholders at a healthcare manufacturer would like to receive feedback on the non-personal activities of particular HCPs. This is illustrated in Figure 7.9. At the right of this figure, the HCP is interacting with a series of touch points, presumably with login-level data which is integrated within a centralized professional database. Different individuals now have alternative information needs:

- The sales representative (illustrated by the sales tablet) wishes to receive information about the professionals within their territory, to help in planning for the next call.

- The regional managers (pictured on the map of the United States), may be interested in summary-level information of non-personal engagement for HCPs within their region, and how this activity complements the personal selling within that region. They would also like to learn about specific activities of some of their most important KOLs, group practice members, and high prescribers.

- At headquarters, sales vice-presidents are interested in national and regional-level activity, to understand the synergies and between personal and non-personal promotion, as well as activities of the most important national accounts. Marketing leaders of brands and therapeutic categories have a similar interest, and also want to learn which of the NPP activities is drawing the deepest engagement and is correlated with incremental sales.

Back to the sales representative, how is the feedback loop implemented to be most valuable? As illustrated in Figure 7.10, the activity of a particular HCP can be automatically generated within the pre-call planning screens associated with that professional. Then, the sales representative can view side by side any correlation or differences between what was shown on the tablet and what the HCP viewed separately on their own volition. With these two data streams summarized, the sales representative can plan an enhanced follow-up call, that:

- Creating a feedback loop across multiple levels to deliver on changes in customer needs and inform future brand and physician interactions

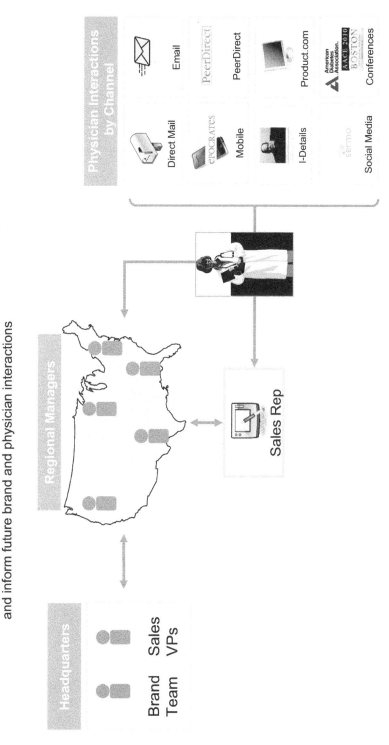

Figure 7.9   Professional relationship marketing measurement is for various stakeholders

- builds on the personal dialogue from the last face-to-face call; and also

- incorporates insights gleaned from the HCP's interactions with non-personal, digital touch points.

Simplified Physician Profile				
Physician	Dr. Samuel Smith		ME #	123456789
Specialty	PCP			
Territory	Chicago North			
Sales Representative	Amber McCallister			
	Product A	Product B	Product C	
Pre-Call Status				
Last Call	4/22/2010			
Slides Completed	50% (slides 1,2,3)			
Topics Presented	Safety and Efficacy			
Topics of Interest	Patient Support Materials			
Other Product Interactions	Visited ProductA.com on 4/20/2010 and learned about clinical trials			
Next Call Suggestions				
Date	4/30/2010			
Slides To Complete	3 Slides			
Topics to Present	Patient Support Materials			
Additional Comments	Invite to lunch and learn			

Weekly Rx Trend Report

	Branded Rx Share	Trend
Product A	3%	Increased
Competitor A1	34%	Decreased
Competitor A2	9%	Increased
Competitor A3	54%	Decreased

Figure 7.10   Feedback loop to sales representative: pre-call planning

What would be particularly noteworthy is when the HCP views online the materials that the sales representative mentioned previously, showing reinforcement of the personal and non-personal channels. Alternatively, perhaps the sales representative is delivering messages primarily about products, and the HCP is exploring other value-added services besides products when navigating through the non-personal, digital channels, and portals. In this way, the manufacturer is presenting a well-rounded set of resources to the practice.

Finally, let us consider how we track the impact of this feedback loop on the sales forces' ability to deliver valuable messages and education? There are multiple mechanisms for doing so, each of which uses a test-control measurement comparison.

- Primary research with the sales representatives themselves, who can report improved access and quality of conversations with their HCPs.

- Primary research with panels of HCPs, who can give improved reports of the value provided by the manufacturer.

- Changes in recorded call activity via the sales tablet, either in time spent or content reviewed.

Correspondingly, we can think about the feedback loop working "in reverse." Using a website content management system, the website content on a PRM portal could be varied to reinforce any specific content covered extensively in presentations made by the sales representative within the laptop. At the time of writing this book, this is conceptual and not actively in practice in the pharmaceutical industry.

Return on Investment for Healthcare Relationship Marketing

In this chapter we will provide an overview of how one can determine the ROI of a RM program. In many regards, this calculation is similar to ROI calculations of any major capital expense. What differs are the specifics related to pharmaceutical products and the need to estimate certain impact quantities.

OVERALL RETURN ON INVESTMENT FRAMEWORK

The basic framework of ROI analysis is shown in Figure 7.11.

$$ROI = (\text{Incremental sales} - \text{Cost}) / \text{Cost}$$

The ROI is measured with respect to a particular time horizon, such as a year or multiple years. Being clear on the time span of the calculation is critical for these reasons:

- infrastructure investments made on new computing infrastructure may be amortized over more than one year;

- incremental sales of patients converted to therapy in this year may continue to accrue in subsequent years, as part of "lifetime value."

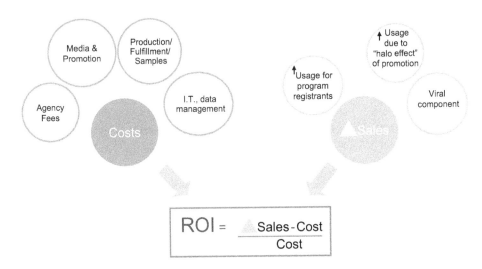

Figure 7.11   Return on Investment Model incorporates cost and sales inputs

ESTIMATING INCREMENTAL SALES

The incremental sales of a CRM program consists of these components:

1. Sum of expected lifetime value of incremental patients on therapy.

2. Added lifetime value to existing patients, through increased adherence.

3. Halo effect of viewing the CRM promotional advertising. This is an estimate that varies based on the therapeutic category and the overall level of media spending. It should be statistically derived. In practice this halo effect has been estimated by healthcare project teams to range from an extra 10 percent of incremental sales to an extra 50 percent.

In the case of PRM, items (1) and (3) have direct correlates, in terms of incremental prescribing of member physicians due to either membership in the PRM program or viewing the advertising associated with the PRM.

In the PRM there is also another potential contributor to incremental sales, and that is the effect of improved sales representative selling as a result of information within the feedback loop. While that is difficult to quantify, the reader is encouraged to find analogues from other sales research projects.

RELATIONSHIP MARKETING PROGRAM COSTS

The items listed here as part of RM program costs apply to both CRM and healthcare RM.

- **Media planning and placement:** these are consulting fees for media agencies to planning, negotiating, and purchasing media, as well as the fees for purchasing the media itself.

- **Communications agency fees:** this includes all costs related to developing campaign materials for each RM phase. Strategic planning and insights for the campaign messages, as well as creative development are included.

- **RM infrastructure:** included are costs of developing and maintaining the database, and necessary software for campaign management and reporting.

- **Data fees:** costs for purchasing or licensing data from third parties, such as list purchases, demographic information, and prescription data.

- **Market research and analytics services:** these are fees for primary market research that supports segmentation or helps in evaluating preliminary creative pieces. The fees include labor for research vendors, honoraria, and facilities. Also included are fees for analytics companies to perform crucial analyses, such as segmentation based on secondary data, as well as campaign tracking, dashboards, optimization, and ROI calculations.

- **Vendor costs:** several other vendors may be involved in operating an RM program, such as call centers, BRC and coupon-processing centers, fulfillment distributors, and other consultants. The fees for each of these separate vendors must be budgeted for and included as costs in the ROI determination.

- **Production:** the cost of physically creating and mass producing volumes of fulfillment materials can be an expensive one for programs that include printed materials. The cost is variable and decreasing with increasing volume and so forecasting estimated quantities is critical in managing costs.

- **Postage:** also for programs with printed fulfillment materials that are required to mail by post, postage is a significant cost at high volumes. A good production consultant can help in managing these using the right paper, envelopes, pre-sorting, and so on. Furthermore, asking channel preference at registration time can reduce printed fulfillment when members choose email delivery. Nonetheless, postage is a budget item should be accounted for. In addition, if direct mail is an acquisition tactic, postal costs will be relevant.

Exercises for Chapter 7

These questions pertain to our running ABC Pharmaceuticals case study and the upcoming launch of the osteoporosis drug ABCOS. See Chapter 5 for details on the promotional plan.

Question 7.1 Calculate program costs of the ABCOS program for the first year in market.

Question 7.2 Calculate expected incremental revenue through new ABCOS patients.

Question 7.3 Calculate increased revenue through extended lifetime value of the thousands of existing patients.

Question 7.4 Assuming a halo effect of 25 percent, what is the 1 year ROI?

Question 7.5 What other intermediate measurements are valuable to collect shortly after launch of the consumer RM program?

8

Optimization and the New Cycle

In Chapter 7 we reviewed a host of techniques and dashboards for measuring and gaining insights into the performance of healthcare relationship marketing (RM) campaigns. In this chapter we will discuss the potential enhancements that marketers should consider implementing as a result of the measurement.

This will be an overview of a wide range of possible healthcare RM optimizations. We will begin at the most concrete, with operational improvements and media adjustments, and proceed throughout the chapter to more abstract decisions, including adjusting segmentations and campaign strategies.

Operational Improvements

Based on measurements of campaign operational processes, multiple improvements can be made which can be organized according to the patient or healthcare professional (HCP) journeys.

- *Acquisition*: if one sees a lower than expected registration rate for multiple promotional tactics, then this may be due to a problem with one of the registration mechanisms. This is a chance to investigate the website registration funnel; is there a peak abandonment page, and can that page be clarified? Is there a high drop-off point during the interactive voice response (IVR) call tree, and can that instruction be clarified, or a step made simpler? Are paper forms such as business reply cards (BRCs) being filled out properly?

- For a PRM program, acquisition also includes a validation step, which may be a back-end ID verification such as an ME# or a state license number, or a follow-up phone call. Whatever process is in place should be checked for effectiveness and timeliness.

- *Conversion*: when consumer relationship marketing (CRM) figures of percentage of patients converting to drug are below expectations, there may be an issue with operations of early trial kits. Instructions on starter kits and early experience kits should be checked for clarity and each step in the process should be examined for drop-off reasons. This holds for both HCPs as well as patients.

- *HCP Trial or Adoption*: if there is minimal gain in a professional relationship marketing (PRM) program, then operationally one would check if product information is displaying optimally on sales tables, on product portals, or within other channels (personal digital assistants (PDAs), webinars, e-details). Also, this is a sign to check for speed and quality of fulfillment on HCP orders of samples, patient literature, and so on.

- *Adherence:* when a CRM programs comes with adherence components there is usually an expected incremental gain over a control group in persistence or compliance. When this lift is not seen, it may be due to operational support issues at a call center or unclear documentation, either printed or online.

Media Optimization

In RM, one is always seeking to reach media that is providing the best direct response of qualified leads. Depending on where the campaign is aiming for in the patient journey, a qualified lead can mean a person highly engaged with activities on a website or with a call center, or a registrant for future CRM or PRM communications.

We have already demonstrated dashboards that can provide insight as to media that is driving the highest number of qualified leads, as well as cost per qualified lead (CPQL). For optimization sake, we can propose the following rule of thumb:

- Among different media sources that are delivering a similar number of qualified leads for a CRM or PRM program, where possible one should optimize and shift one's spending and purchase more toward that media source with a lower CPQL.

Note that this rule rests on the assumption that more of the efficient media source can be purchased and with similar expected response rates. The rule also states we are optimizing among options delivering similar numbers of leads, such as two magazines to the same demographic, or two health portal content areas within the same condition. It would be non-optimal to shift money to an efficient but low-volume lead provider (tens of leads) from a somewhat less efficient, high-volume lead provider (returning hundreds of leads).

Also worthy of consideration are the branding effects of different media sources, especially during the launch and growth phases of a healthcare product where branding is important. Brand awareness and brand recognition effects of media are best measured via primary research studies that specifically ask about media sources of awareness. Thus, if branding is important for a campaign, and it can be shown that a slightly less efficient media tactic is proven to provide enhanced brand awareness, that media tactic is probably worth retaining. However, do not fall into a trap of equating as "branding" the raw counts of Internet impressions, print circulations, or mass media gross ratings points. These are prone to encourage overstatement, as not all people exposed to a medium actually consume it. Just think of unopened newspapers or magazines, commercials not seen due to bathroom breaks, or banner ads unnoticed. Sure, for effective media placements, wider circulations or higher impression counts are desirable. Yet, to assess and validate branding effects, primary research is best.

Promotional Tactical Changes

Aside from merely the media tactics, there may also be situations to reconsider other touch points throughout the cadence in either a CRM or PRM program. If a particular feature is not being selected by the target segments, despite high overall RM participation, that may point to an executed tactic that is not relevant.

For example, say there is a particular mechanism of action video describing how a medication works, and is intended for high-prescribing physicians in the therapeutic category. Thus mechanism of action (MOA) video might be placed on the product website, within e-details, and within the sales representatives' tablets. Yet across all these tactics, it is rarely seen or utilized.

In these cases, the alternatives are to:

1. remove the tactic altogether, feeling the functionality is not really needed by the intended audience to make prescribing decisions;

2. modify the execution, create a different version of this tactic (the video) with the same clinical content but a fresh presentation. Then retest this revision in focus group market research and, if favorable, re-release in market.

Option (2) should only be chosen if there is strong conviction in the necessity of the tactic or the latest research is quite favorable.

Favoring Test Outcomes

In Chapter 5, as we developed the analytics strategy for RM, we strongly advised in-market testing where there are multiple alternatives. For example, alternative banner ad executions within the acquisition phase of a CRM program.

When the results come back from the in-market test, if there is a clear leader among the options in response rate, engagement, or user feedback, then it is incumbent to select the best option and remove the others. In future campaigns, additional refinements may come from other in-market tests.

Adjusting Segmentation

We have spoken in previous chapters about designing an RM segmentation and then implementing a brief survey at registration to assign people to segments; then members of each segment can be presented with customized content. Thus, physicians interested more in building a practice may have different options featured in a PRM portal than those primarily interested in learning about new products.

However, occasionally the registration tallies may not match your research segmentation ratios. Or what if the behaviors of each segment are counterintuitive to your prediction? In this case there may be a need to re-evaluate the segmentation. First, review the latest secondary data and revise the market research if necessary. Second, reanalyze the data and develop a modified list of segments. Finally, cast a critical eye as to which of the segments has the most upside opportunity for RM.

Rethinking the Campaign Strategy

In the rare scenarios where there is minimal response rate and engagement for an in-market RM program, there may be a need to reconsider the strategy of the campaign. Why might this happen? The marketplace may have changed significantly, as happens with the launch of new competitors, for example.

In these instances, it is critical to go back to discovery, reconsider who the target segments are, and refresh the primary and secondary research on those segments. Only after regaining a firm understanding of the motivations, preferences, and barriers of the target can one then move on to developing a new RM strategy and design.

9

Conclusions and the Future

In this final chapter we review the primary messages of this textbook, as they stand in 2011, and then point to trends that may evolve in the future. We also provide advice for other ways to stay current and informed about healthcare relationship marketing (RM).

Tactics Come and Go, But Strategies Endure

As the writing of this book came to a close, it became apparent that only some of the specific consumer and promotional tactics available in 2011 were fully described in detail here. Rather, even in the chapters on strategy and execution of campaigns, we have tended to keep out descriptions at the categorical level: multi-channel touch points, e-details, or acquisition vehicles. This book has not served as an actual catalogue of the latest (as of 2011) particular techniques and vendors that can be plugged into in a consumer relationship marketing (CRM) or professional relationship marketing (PRM) program.

While briefly feeling chagrin, the author feels that this may in fact be for the best. Had we aimed to list most every CRM or PRM component, we may have missed several, and some we may have listed would fall out of favor due to ineffectiveness within a year or two. Far more important is understanding the principles of RM: strategy, segments, personas, experience maps, promotional planning, communication touch points, measurement, and optimization. With these principles, readers should be able to understand the criteria for reviewing and selecting their own in-market tactics, after designing the program that meets the company's brand or portfolio objectives.

The Present and Future

A TIME OF FLUX

If there was a recurring theme throughout this book, it was this: now is a moment of great flux in healthcare marketing, both for consumers and professionals.

The move to multi-channel, digital and mobile communications, with user-generated content and communities, was not imaginable in 2005 but is a reality in 2010. Government regulations in these new channels are evolving. Success metrics are multi-faceted and non-standard.

What is an example of how the healthcare CRM changes are happening before our eyes? A recent *New York Times* article (Singer 2010) called out two social media websites that encourage consumers to describe their medical conditions and what treatments they have been using. The positive aspects of websites like these include:

- encouragement to patients to track their progress toward achieving health goals, such as weight loss;

- providing another venue for desperate patients with serious conditions to quickly link to others who are suffering similarly, and learning about potential treatments;

- potentially serving as an input to development of personalized medicine.

However, there are also negative aspects to this ad-hoc, user-generated compendium. One point of concern is that the self-reported condition and treatment data, along with efficacy ratings by patients, are anonymized, aggregated, and reported to the website membership as if they were outcomes measures. They are even being sold to pharmaceutical companies as market research. There is great potential for self-reporting bias and inaccuracies, as these combined social media results will have neither the rigor nor accuracy of clinical trials or formal market research.

A BRIEF INDUSTRY EXPERT VIEW

We have also asked one of our industry experts, Mark Taylor, to comment on the future of pharmaceutical RM, and how in the next decade it will change from the paradigms of the last ten to 20 years. His summary comments are progressive and optimistic:

> *Pharmaceutical marketing will begin to grow up in the next decade. It will start to realize that by combining marketing messaging with true consumer utility it can really be the most impactful industry. The industry will further learn that multi-channel, multi-level approaches work best. It will move from a passive position to a much more proactive reaching out to consumers with value (utility) as the incentive to engage. Social media, hampered by industry regulations and more hampered by industry conservatism will find its legs and be an incredibly important element of the mix for pharmaceutical marketers and their consumers alike.*

Keeping Up to Date

In writing a textbook that I hope will endure for several years, this dynamic landscape is a challenge. The way we've handled this changing environment is threefold:

1.   I have aimed to present a solid foundation for RM rooted in constructs that will not soon change: the patient journey, the physician journey, segmentation, and a cadence based on moments of decision making. These are constants that should last despite changes in technology.

2.   I am continually writing about the latest developments in my blog, called Healthcare Relationship Marketing, and found at this URL http://healthcarerm.blogspot.com. Everyone is welcome to come and read about the latest technology and communications trends, and how they apply to healthcare. Please offer comments as well.

3.   We encourage the reader to keep abreast of the latest healthcare industry, CRM technology, and digital news. One can subscribe to RSS feeds, Twitter updates, or emailed summaries from leading industry sources like:

- Medical Marketing and Media

- Med Ad News

- Pharmaceutical Executive

- CRM Today

- Direct Marketing News

- Tech Crunch

- Media Post

- Manhattan Research

- Forrester

With all of these recommendations, this author sincerely hopes that the reader has found our journey together valuable, reviewing the discovery, design and evaluation of RM programs. We hope the issues, challenges, and solutions presented here can serve as a foundation for years to come.

Appendix A: Solutions to Exercises

In this Appendix we provide solutions to the exercises at the end of each chapter, all related to our case study of the fictitious company ABC Pharmaceuticals, and the launch and subsequent relationship marketing (RM) programs for their fictitious osteoporosis drug ABCOS. Note that there may be multiple answers to each question, and nearly every question has solutions at varying levels of depth. Generally, with these solutions we will provide general answers and suggestions as to how to find more specifics.

Chapter 2 Exercises

Question 2.1   Who are the target consumers for ABCOS? What stages of the patient journey are most of these consumers at with respect to ABCOS?

The target consumers are female patients who have been diagnosed with osteoporosis, primarily in the age range of 45 to 70. These patients may either be in the diagnosis or the treatment stages of the patient journey. For those in the diagnosis stage, at first receiving the diagnosis of osteoporosis, the patient should be aware of ABCOS and consider speaking to their physician about it. For those in the treatment stage, ABCOS may be worthy of discussion with the physician as an alternative therapy to switch to, particularly for those patients that are not staying adherent on existing therapies.

Question 2.2   Who are the target healthcare professionals (HCPs) for ABCOS? What stages of the physician journey are most of these professionals at with respect to ABCOS?

The target HCPs included the highest prescribers in the osteoporosis category, both primary care physicians and specialists. The specialists include gynecologists, orthopedists, rheumatologists, and endocrinologists. We anticipate that the office staffs of these professionals will also be a target, because prior authorization and pharmacy interactions may be required when patients prescribed ABCOS are filling their prescriptions.

Question 2.3   What are the core components of the consumer RM system that must be developed for ABCOS?

Core components of the consumer relationship marketing (CRM) system for ABCOS include:

- Acquisition media, across multiple media channels to raise awareness of ABCOS, and to encourage patients to sign up for more information, to speak to their physicians about ABCOS.

- A patient starter kit that describes the innovative mechanism of action, the delivery mechanism, states how to administer, and what to expect.

- Tools to manage bone and joint health, and track health and lifestyle changes.

- A financial assistance program for patients to help conversion to drug, because we anticipate a new drug in a crowded therapeutic class will have Third Tier formulary status at best.

Question 2.4   What are the core components of the healthcare professional RM system that must be developed for ABCOS?

Core components of professional relationship marketing (PRM) should include:

- Awareness and acquisition across multiple media sources including sales force with tablets, e-detailing, key opinion leaders (KOLs) discussing the efficacy data, and instructions for administration.

- Space at relevant specialty medical conventions.

- A trial program encouraging physicians to try ABCOS on several patients and collecting survey results after treatment for several months.

- Management of cost and coverage-related issues within the office practice, because osteoporosis is a crowded category with orals, branded and generics, and prior authorizations, and step edits are anticipated.

Chapter 3 Exercises

Question 3.1   What relevant prescription data should be gathered to help understand the market dynamics relevant to ABCOS? What are the relevant specialties?

It would be worthwhile to study monthly prescription trends in the osteoporosis category, both NRx and TRx. Note that this is a crowded therapeutic category that includes generics as well as branded medications, orals and non-orals, and daily dose versus extended dosing.

Prescribing levels and patterns by specialty within the osteoporosis category would also be important, to help prioritize among the specialties for sales force coverage. Even prescriber-level data would be beneficial to understand which physicians were early adopters of other innovative medications in this category. ABC Pharmaceuticals should also consider other more behavioral segmentations, like physicians who exhibit loyalty to certain brands, or those who were early adopters of previously new osteoporosis medications.

Furthermore, anonymous *patient-level data* trends would be valuable to review for several reasons. First, we can establish a baseline for source of business metrics in the osteoporosis category, like monthly new patient starts and switching from one medication to another. Secondly, patient-level data can help establish the definitive target age range for women taking osteoporosis medications. Finally, we can evaluate the shape of the persistence drop-off curve, particularly the daily medications, for ABCOS aims to improve upon that curve.

Question 3.2   What market research should ABC Pharmaceuticals be conducting related to the osteoporosis category. Consider both consumer research and HCP research.

Research with consumers can help uncover their journey, marked by pain, of managing osteoporosis, what medications have been taken, and what specialists have been consulted. Research may reveal to what extent people seek an extended timeline between dosing. The research can also help understand, and then size, the patient interest in non-oral medications, and those lasting more than one day, even up to months.

For HCPs, research can help understand and quantify the likelihood to prescribe non-oral treatments, and those with long durations of effects. Quantitative research can also breakdown this likelihood to prescribe by specialty.

Question 3.3   How can we better understand the online behaviors of consumers in the osteoporosis market in general, and what might that teach us to plan for the ABCOS CRM launch?

As described in Chapter 3, search engine frequency analysis by category can uncover the terminology patients use when searching for information on osteoporosis and when they are seeking treatments. Social media analysis will help uncover the language that patients use to describe the pain of osteoporosis, the benefits of medications, and any shortcomings they may have with current medications.

Social media analysis on HCP communities may uncover how physicians feel about current osteoporosis therapies and unmet needs in medication currently available.

Question 3.4   What forecasting may be relevant to the upcoming launch of ABCOS?

In advance of this new product launch, a review of the competitive pipelines within osteoporosis treatments would help identify how other recently launched medications have fared, especially others that are non-oral, and with monthly or longer duration of effect. The pipeline review can also identify the depth of competition in the category in years ahead and which medications may go generic. Analogues may be another forecasting tool; to assess the peak market share of other drugs in crowded markets with innovative delivery mechanisms.

Question 3.5   ABC Pharmaceuticals wants to understand if it has the operational capabilities for CRM and PRM. ABC has sales force databases and reporting systems, and has sent email and direct mail to physicians in the past. They have also once piloted a consumer copay discount offer for another product. What are the different operational and infrastructure considerations that ABC Pharmaceuticals must face for CRM and PRM related to the ABCOS campaigns?

ABC Pharmaceuticals should definitely partake in an operational needs assessment to determine what infrastructure is required for RM. For consumer

RM, ABC will want the capability to capture names of patients who wish to find out more about ABCOS, or who take advantage of cost assistance. From a professional standpoint, ABC Pharmaceuticals will engage in non-personal promotion to extend the reach of the 300-person sales force and to reach professionals at additional channels, to communicate from KOLs the clinical benefits of ABCOS.

Chapter 4 Exercises

Question 4.1 What market research with consumers can be designed for developing a strategy around the launch of the ABCOS CRM program?

Consumer market research can be conducted on sufferers of osteoporosis, asking about the various stages of their patient journeys. First qualitative research, either with focus groups or individually, can step through what the patients have experienced from initial symptoms, to seeking information, visits to HCPs, diagnosis, and treatment. This qualitative research will raise common themes and frequently mentioned issues, the specifics of which can be determined with follow-up quantitative research.

The strategy around the launch of a CRM program should be rooted in helping patients make key decisions along their journey. In a new product launch, the key decisions to accelerate are seeking more information, visiting a HCP, obtaining diagnosis, and starting treatment.

Students are encouraged to develop sample scripts for qualitative research, as well as screening criteria and multiple-choice questions for quantitative research.

Question 4.2 What media channels might be appropriate for the target osteoporosis patients who would take ABCOS?

This question should be answered via a thorough media consumption analysis, covering all channels including television, print, and digital. Certainly, there is a distinctive target demographic of post-menopausal women, typically 55 and older. There are certainly focused print publications, television stations and shows aimed at this demographic, with corresponding digital properties. In addition, there are opportunities for targeting media investments related to the osteoporosis category, on website health portals, health publications, or documentaries. Finally, paid search may be quite viable for the media plan and this should be verified with a quantitative analysis on monthly search frequencies, as described in Chapter 4.

Question 4.3   How could creative elements of the CRM program demonstrate empathy for the osteoporosis patients who would take ABCOS?

There are multiple approaches that creative can take to seem empathetic. A few are:

- creative can highlight the struggles and pain of the osteoporosis patient;

- alternatively, the creative images and messaging may illustrate what activities osteoporosis patients are missing out on, or where they are making compromises;

- another approach, further down the patient cycle, is to illustrate how the osteoporosis patient is seeking a HCP's advice, or obtaining treatment.

Chapter 5 Exercises

Question 5.1   How are the consumer objectives for ABCOS being met by the media mix? Comment on the relative mix of digital versus print media, and whether this is appropriate for the disease category and the consumer demographic.

The media mix chosen for the ABCOS consumer launch is evenly spread across channels and positions a broad range of demographically targeted properties. Print, television, and Internet are all aimed at women over 40 years old. After the campaign launches, advertising awareness and direct response performance should both be tracked to determine which channel was most impactful.

Question 5.2   What are the business objectives for PRM and how well are the tactical suggestions meeting those?

The objectives at a new product launch are spreading product awareness and stimulating product trial among the high-prescribing, early adopting physicians. The tactics listed (conventions, electronic journals, sales force, Doc Alerts) are a broad approach toward achieving that reach. Another item to consider: non-personal tele-details or e-Details can usually be implemented in a targeted fashion, matching to one's own target list.

Question 5.3   Develop a learning plan for the ABCOS CRM.

Below is an example of an ABCOS 2012 Consumer RM Campaign: Learning and Optimization Plan.

The reader is encouraged to review and make more specific if they wish.

Subject	Objective	Metrics for Success	Data and Measurement Tools	Marketing Decisions and Implications
1) Increase Awareness of ABCOS	Will the CRM campaign increase awareness of ABCOS?	Increased ABCOS brand awareness versus before campaign	ATU study on ABCOS and advertising awareness	Further advertising investment, especially those promoting awareness and branding
2) Gather Responses into the ABCOS CRM DB for future contacts	What is the most cost-effective way of gathering leads into DB for future dialogue?	Response and registration volumes and rates for each media source. Questionnaire responses for qualified rules: women ages 40–65	Response data, and cost per lead by channel. Website and call center registration rates	Investment decisions by channel: DRTV, print, direct mail, and so on. Improve website and/or call center to increase acquisition rates
3) Increase new patient starts on ABCOS	Has the CRM campaign brought more new patients started on ABCOS?	Likelihood to ask doctor for ABCOS from non-patients. Rx measures of responders becoming ABCOS patients Actual ABCOS Rx usage among registrants	ATU tracking study Patient-level longitudinal claims data; NRx share. Self-reported usage question from responders	Continue or re-craft messages and media of campaign accordingly

Question 5.4 Develop a learning plan for the ABCOS PRM program.

The reader should use the format outlined in Chapter 5, and specific to the ABCOS HCP Promotional Plan.

Question 5.5 Given the promotional planning for ABCOS CRM that was spelled out at the end of Chapter 5, what is a range of response rates that might be expected for each tactic? What is the range of the grand total of CRM registrations responses that we might expect?

This question is a mini-project in itself and our aim here is to direct the reader with guidelines on how to develop a solution. Before giving a response to this question, it is worth mentioning a few caveats:

- It is best to consult a reference guide of recent response rates, such as the Direct Marketing Association Response Rate Trends Report (DMA 09) or an Internet set of campaign experiences within your company.

- Response rates can change over the years. At the time of writing this book (in 2010) they have generally been decreasing over recent years due to the clutter of direct mail and email. Thus, recent benchmarks should take precedent in forming estimations.

- Your response rate estimates should always include a range, not only for responding through to the website or call center registration stage, but also for the verified registration itself.

- Response rates of direct mail and email are usually higher with a customer list than with a list of purchased prospects.

- Several factors aside from the media channel determine the response rate, including creative and messaging execution, as well as the perceived value exchange of the offer and the program.

That being said, here are some estimated ranges for response rates the reader may wish to use:

- direct mail: 1–3 percent (higher for current customer lists);

- email: 5–20 percent open rate; 10–30 percent click through rate (of those opened); those rates are multiplied to get to a website landing page;

- banners: 0.1–0.5 percent of impressions will click through to a website landing page;

- search engines: 0.3–1 percent of impressions will get to a website landing page;

- direct response television (DRTV): Highly variable; responses come into either a call center or a website; a weekly range of calls or website visits may be 50 to several hundred, while the ad runs, or course depending on gross rating points (GRPs);

- print: variable; responses come to website, call center, or via business reply cards (BRCs) (effective for print) a total of 0.1–1 percent of circulation may register. For simplicity sake, presume the magazines each have a circulation between 200,000 and 500,000 readers monthly (actual figures probably available online).

As for registration itself, please note that most direct response acquisition tactics have a two-step process: first drive to the destination (such as landing page or interactive voice response (IVR) script), and then have visitors complete a registration form. The second part has its own drop-off, with a range of 3 to 20 percent for healthcare possible; professional RM programs tend to have higher registration completion rates than consumer programs.

As a follow up, the reader is encouraged to develop a table of low and high response rates based upon the estimates above and the media based on the media mix provided at the end of this chapter. The format should be like this:

Tactic	Cost	Reach/ Impressions	Response Rate Low	Response Rate High	Registrants Low	Registrants High	Cost Per Registrant (Low/High)
DRTV1							
DRTV2							
Print 1							
Print 2							
...							
Total							

For extra credit, consider what the overlap in registrants may be among promotional sources and how the notion of "qualified lead" may change your calculations.

Chapter 6 Exercises

Question 6.1   For the media plan outlined at the end of Chapter 5 on the ABCOS CRM launch, what source coding and data transmission issues must be addressed?

For the online media sources (banners, search, email), one should insure there is tagging so that click through to the website can be tracked by source, and URL parameter passing to insure tracking all the way to registration. For offline media, there should be separate vanity URLs redirecting to the website and separate toll-free numbers going to the IVR system, separated by source. BRCs from print sources should be coded so that the data entry vendor may code these appropriately to track leads by source.

As extra credit, the student should consider crafting a *source code matrix,* that maps each acquisition media channel to a source code, URL, toll-free number, and other relevant information.

Question 6.2   Design a simple contact stream of three communications for patient registrants of the ABCOS CRM program. Highlight any specific business rules that should be activated to trigger those contacts.

Upon registration, it would be valuable to include a brief survey that can be used for segmentation: the questions might be based on current osteoporosis (or pain) medications being taken, specialty of physician the patient is seeing, and patient versus caregiver. Channel preference can also be asked, to determine whether the registrant prefers printed or electronic communications. Of course, an opt-in question should also be added to the registration to gain permission for follow-up communications.

Then the start of a contact stream can be as follows:

1.   Acknowledgement and welcome communication: sent after registration is received; summarizing the benefits of the ABCOS program and reminding what future communications will be coming.

2.   There can be a split based on medication history for the second
      mailer:

      a)   for untreated patients, information on available therapies,
            information about ABCOS, and a doctor discussion guide;

      b)   for competitive patients, information about ABCOS;

      c)   for ABCOS current users, a piece about managing expectations
            with the product, and a tracking diary.

3.   An osteoporosis health management piece, say one to two months
      later, for all registrants, which may have components varied based
      upon treatment status and specialty seen. In this piece, a question
      may be asked to update medication status.

There would be more to the contact stream, linked to untreated patients
converting to ABCOS and managing current ABCOS patients to encourage
persistence. Also worth noting is delivery of content based on channel
preference. For extra credit, the student should develop diagrams of this flow.

Chapter 7 Exercises

We recommend the student work through these examples in an extended
spreadsheet, with separate tabs for costs, incremental revenue, and return on
investment. The itemization is spelled out based on the components of the
section "Return on Investment for Healthcare Relationship Marketing." The
details of the CRM program costs are detailed in the section "Continuing Case
Study with ABC Pharmaceuticals and ABCOS" in Chapter 5.

To answer the questions below, we need to make some simplified
assumptions regarding program performance within the first year. Each of
these figures can be parameters with low and high estimates within a return on
investment (ROI) calculation:

*   100,000 unique, qualified registrants into the consumer RM
    database;

*   80,000 of them not on ABCOS, 20,000 of them already taking
    ABCOS;

- overall channel preference of 50 percent digital, 50 percent paper-based;

- 30 percent of ABCOS CRM registrants previously not on ABCOS convert to ABCOS;

- 5 percent of a matched sample control group convert to ABCOS;

- Of those 30 percent converting, the average utilization of copay assistance was $25;

- $700 estimated lifetime value per new ABCOS user;

- $200 incremental value per ABCOS CRM registrant versus placebo;

- Average of $20 in printing and postage for printed cadence materials;

- $500,000 total development costs for all program materials.

Question 7.1 Calculate program costs of the ABCOS program for the first year in market.

Media costs are spelled out individually in the section "Continuing Case Study with ABC Pharmaceuticals and ABCOS" in Chapter 5 as are agency and vendor fees. CRM database infrastructure costs are also included in this section, and those may be amortized over several years. Other costs include production and postage of materials. This is calculated based on the 50,000 individuals with preference of printed materials, times the average of $20, or $1,000,000. Another cost is the copay financial reimbursement, of 24,000 members * $25 = $600,000.

Question 7.2 Calculate expected incremental revenue through new ABCOS patients.

Using the above performance estimates, this is 80,000 * 25% * $700 = $14 Million. Note the 25 percent is based on a difference of conversion between the CRM registrants and the control group.

Question 7.3 Calculate increased revenue through extended lifetime value of the thousands of existing patients.

There are 20,000 current ABCOS patients, with an average incremental gain of $200 versus the control group. This product is $4 million.

Question 7.4 Assuming a halo effect of 25percent, what is the 1 year ROI?

The halo effect is typically multiplied by the incremental revenue for acquisition. This can mean taking the $14 million and multiplying by 125 percent to get $17.5 million. Then add the $4 million from adherence lift to get $21.5 million of incremental sales.

Then using the costs from question 7.1, calculate ROI as:

$$(\$21.5 \text{ million} - \text{Cost}) / \text{Cost}$$

Your result should be a positive return, and significantly greater than one, meaning more than a doubling of the investment.

Note that with increasing registration volumes, the fixed costs remain constant while smaller variable costs increase, and the ROI grows higher.

Question 7.5 What other intermediate measurements are valuable to collect shortly after launch of the consumer RM program?

Click through rates of banner advertisements will give a measure of awareness and branding effects. Website click stream analysis will reveal interest levels in attributes of ABCOS, as well as the effectiveness of the registration funnel. Similarly, reviewing the call center inputs and the IVR responses will gauge effectiveness of the phone response funnels.

Market research should also be conducted to gauge brand awareness lifts from the CRM program and its component advertising.

Bibliography

Alreck, P.R., and Settle, R.B., *The Survey Research Handbook*, Third Edition, McGraw-Hill, 2003.

Arnold, M., "SanofiIPone App Offers Diabetics Carb Counting," *Medical Marketing and Media,* vol. 45, no. 1, January 2010, p. 24.

Arnold, M., "Europe Edges US in Social Media for Health Info, says study," *Medical Marketing and Media,* online version, March 25, 2010.

Baron, R., and Sissors, J., *Media Planning*, Seventh Edition, McGraw-Hill, 2010.

Burby, J., and Atkinson, S., *Actionable Web Analytics*, Wiley, 2007.

Chase, J., and Iskowitz, M., "Data Crunch," *Medical Marketing and Media,* vol. 45, no. 3, March 2010, pp. 34–38.

Comer, B., "Friending Social Media," *Medical Marketing and Media,* vol. 45, no. 2, February 2010, pp. 36–39.

Cook, A., *Forecasting for the Pharmaceutical Industry,* Gower Publishing, 2006.

Creswell, J.W., *Research Design: Qualitative, Quantitative, and Mixed Methods Approaches*, Sage Publications, 2009.

Davenport, T.H., and Harris, J.G., *Competing on Analytics: The New Science of Winning*, Harvard Business School Press, 2007.

Dean, A.M., and Voss, D., *Design and Analysis of Experiments* (Springer Texts in Statistics), Springer, 1998.

Dillon, W.R., and Goldstein, M., *Multivariate Analysis: Methods and Applications*, John Wiley & Sons, 1984.

Direct Marketing Asssociation (DMA), DMA 2009 Response Rate Trends Report, DMA Press, 2009.

Duda, R.O., Hart, P.E., and Stork, D.G., *Pattern Classification*, Second Edition, John Wiley & Sons, 2001.

Eckes, G., *General Electric's Six Sigma Revolution: How General Electric and Others Turned Process Into Profits*, John Wiley & Sons, 2001.

Edison Research, "Twitter Usage In America: 2010," The Edison Research/ Arbitron Internet and Multimedia Study, 2010.

Elkin, N., "How America Searches, Health and Wellness," (survey conducted by Opinion Research Corporation), *iCrossing,* January 2008.

Forrester Research, North American Consumer Technology Adoption Study (NACTAS) 2006 Benchmark Survey, Q4 2006.

Giegerich, M., "Busting Silos," *Medical Marketing and Media,* vol. 45, no. 1, January 2010, pp. 48–49.

Gorchels, L., *The Product Manager's Handbook: The Complete Product Management Resource,* Third Edition, McGraw-Hill, 2005.

Haimowitz, I., "Healthcare Relationship Marketing," blog since 2010, http://healthcarerm.blogspot.com/.

Haimowitz, I. and Obata, C., "The Science of Eavesdropping," *Medical Marketing and Media,* vol. 44, no. 5, May 2009, pp. 57–59.

Han, J., and Kamber, M., *Data Mining: Concepts and Techniques,* Second Edition, Morgan Kaufmann, 2006.

Iskowitz, M., "Docs prefer E-detailing slightly less in 2009," *Medical Marketing and Media,* vol. 45, no. 2, February 2010, p. 26.

Iskowitz, M., "DTC spend up 4% on launches, aging blockbusters, says Kantar" *Medical Marketing and Media* (online version), March 17, 2010.

Kaushal, R., Kern, L.M., Barrón, Y., Quaresimo, J., and Abramson, E. "Electronic Prescribing Improves Medication Safety in Community-Based Office Practices," *Journal of General Internal Medicine,* vol. 25, no. 6, February 2010, pp. 530–536.

Kaushik, A., *Web Analytics, An Hour a Day,* Wiley, 2007

L2 (Luxury Lab) and PhD Media, "Digital IQ Index: Pharma," online report, May 2010.

Lam, M., "Psychographic Demonstration: Segmentation Studies Prepare to Prove Teir Worth," *Pharmaceutical Executive,* January 2004.

Loftus, B., "Using Diaries, Calendars, and Technology to Improve Headache Care," *Practical Neurology,* vol.8, no.9, November/December 2009, pp. 26–29.

Loftus, P., "Pfizer Adds New Type of Tablet to Sales Calls," *Wall Street Journal,* December 15, 2009, p. B4.

Martin, T.W., "More Doctors are Prescribing Medicines Online," *The Wall Street Journal,* April 20, 2010, p. D2.

Monari, G.L., "CRM Builds Bonds in Cardio," *Med Ad News,* vol. 29, no. 2, February 2010, pp. 18–19.

National Community Pharmacists Association, "Take as Directed: A Prescription Not Followed," Research Conducted by The Polling Company. December 15, 2006.

National Council on Patient Information and Education, "Enhancing Prescription Medicine Adherence: A National Action Plan," August 2006.

Nielsen, J., *Designing Web Usabiity,* New Riders Publishing, 1999.

Nielsen, J., and Tahir, M., *Homepage Usability: 50 Websites Deconstructed,* New Riders Publishing, 2002.

Oakland, J.S., *Statistical Process Control,* Sixth Edition, Elsevier, 2008.

Prochaska, J.O., Norcross, J., and DiClemente, C.C., *Changing for Good*, Harper Collins, 1994.

Shalo, S., "Marketing by the Numbers," *Pharmaceutical Executive*, July 2002.

Sharma, S., and Schwartz, S. (interview), "Reinventing the Market Research Function," *Pharmaceutical Executive*, vol. 30, no. 1, January 2010, pp. 46–51.

Singer, N., "When Patients Meet Online, Are There Side Effects?," *The New York Times* (online), May 28, 2010.

SK&A, "Physician Access: U.S. Physicians' Availability to See Drug and Device Sales Reps," research by SK&A, a Cegedim Company, February 2010.

Stagnitti, M., "Comparing Population Characteristics of Persons Purchasing Prescribed Drugs from Mail Order Pharmacies with Persons Purchasing Prescribed Drugs from Other Outlets, 2005," Statistical Brief 200, Agency for Healthcare Research and Quality, February, 2008.

Stone, B., and Jacobs, R., *Successful Direct Marketing Methods*, McGraw Hill, 2008.

Tenaglia, M., and Meister, C., "First, Do No Harm: Designing and Deploying Company Copay Offset Programs without Devaluing the Brand," *Pharmaceutical Executive*, vol. 30, no.1, January 2010, pp. 38–44.

Todman, C., *Designing a Data Warehouse: Supporting Customer Relationship Management*, Hewlett-Packard Professional Books, 2000.

Tolve, A., "Emerging wireless solutions for patient compliance," *Eye for Pharma* online, January 12, 2010.

Vecchione, A., "The Online Rep," *Medical Marketing and Media*, vol.44, no. 11, November 2009, pp. 36–40.

Vittal, S., "The Listening Platform Landscape: New Solutions Extend Beyond Tracking To Deliver Consumer Insights," Forrester Research report, January 22, 2009.

Wei, W.S., *Time Series Analysis: Univariate and Multivariate Methods*, Second Edition, Addison Wesley, 2005.

Wunderman, L.A., *Being Direct: Making Advertising Pay*, Direct Marketing Association, 2004.

Websites Cited Throughout the Book

CONSUMER

Daily Strength social network   http://www.dailystrength.org/

Patients Like Me social network   http://www.patientslikeme.com/

PROFESSIONAL

Medscape portal and social network   http://www.medscape.com

Sermo social network   http://www.sermo.com

Ozmosis social network   http://www.ozmosis.com

INDUSTRY ORGANIZATIONS

Pharmaceutical Management Science Association   http://www.pmsa.net

Pharmaceutical Market Research Group   http://www.pmrg.org

Index